BIZ MACKEY,
A GIANT BEHIND THE PLATE

◆ ◆ ◆

Tales from the Philadelphia Phillies Dugout: A Collection of the Greatest Phillies Stories Ever Told, 1st, 2nd, and 3rd eds.

Native Sons: Philadelphia Baseball Players Who Made the Major Leagues

Mickey Vernon: The Gentleman First Baseman

Veterans Stadium: Field of Memories

Phillies Essential: Everything You Need to Know to Be a Real Fan!

The Mogul: Eddie Gottlieb, Philadelphia Sports Legend and Pro Basketball Pioneer

The Fightin' Phils: Oddities, Insights, and Untold Stories

Philadelphia Phillies: Past and Present

Back Again: The Story of the 2009 Phillies

Shibe Park–Connie Mack Stadium

Philadelphia's Top 50 Baseball Players

Great Stuff: Baseball's Most Amazing Pitching Feats

The Champions of Philadelphia: The Greatest Eagles, Phillies, Sixers, and Flyers Teams

Biz Mackey

A GIANT BEHIND THE PLATE

The Story of the Negro League Star
and Hall of Fame Catcher

◆ ◆ ◆

RICH WESTCOTT

◆ ◆ ◆

Forewords by **MONTE IRVIN**
and **RAY C. MACKEY III**

TEMPLE UNIVERSITY PRESS
Philadelphia ◆ *Rome* ◆ *Tokyo*

TEMPLE UNIVERSITY PRESS
Philadelphia, Pennsylvania 19122
www.temple.edu/tempress

Text design by Kate Nichols

Library of Congress Cataloging-in-Publication Data

Names: Westcott, Rich, author.
Title: Biz Mackey, a giant behind the plate : the story of the Negro league
    star and Hall of Fame catcher / Rich Westcott.
Description: Philadelphia, Pennsylvania : Temple University Press, 2018. |
    Includes bibliographical references and index.
Identifiers: LCCN 2017035622 (print) | LCCN 2017048875 (ebook) | ISBN
    9781439915530 (E-book) | ISBN 9781439915516 (hardback : alk. paper)
Subjects: LCSH: Mackey, Biz, 1897–1965. | Catchers (Baseball)—United
    States—Biography. | Baseball players—United States—Biography. | African
    American baseball players—Biography. | African American baseball
    managers—Biography. | Negro leagues—United States—History. |
    Baseball—United States—History—20th century. | BISAC: SPORTS &
    RECREATION / Baseball / History. | HISTORY / United States / State &
    Local / Middle Atlantic (DC, DE, MD, NJ, NY, PA). | BIOGRAPHY &
    AUTOBIOGRAPHY / Women.
Classification: LCC GV865.M219 (ebook) | LCC GV865.M219 W47 2018
    (print) | DDC 796.357092 [B] —dc23
LC record available at https://lccn.loc.gov/2017035622

Printed in the United States of America

9 8 7 6 5 4 3 2 1

♦ ♦ ♦

TO ALL THE AFRICAN AMERICAN BASEBALL PLAYERS who were denied the chance to join white players in Major League Baseball because of the unforgivable racist barriers in place at the time, I dedicate this book to you and the memories you left behind. As Biz Mackey and others clearly demonstrated, you had just as much to give as your white brothers, a fact that was at long last fully substantiated when the integration of baseball finally became a reality. Now, some 70 years later, I salute you for your contributions to baseball history and for laying the groundwork for those who came after you.

♦ ♦ ♦

CONTENTS

◆ ◆ ◆

CONTENTS

FOREWORD BY MONTE IRVIN

◆ ◆ ◆

O f all those who participated in the Negro Leagues during the first half of the 20th century, there was no one quite like Biz Mackey. As a player, as a manager, and as a personality, he was in a class by himself.

As a player, Mackey ranks among the greatest catchers of all time. In the Negro Leagues, Josh Gibson was a better hitter, but Biz was a better catcher. Overall, Biz was most like Bill Dickey in terms of all-around ability. He belongs in a class with Dickey, Mickey Cochrane, Roy Campanella, Yogi Berra, and Johnny Bench—baseball's greatest catchers.

Although he was an outstanding hitter, Mackey was strongest as a receiver. There wasn't any part of catching that he didn't master. He had an exceptionally accurate throwing arm, he was skilled at blocking the plate, he could block the ball in the dirt, and he never dropped a pop-up. He was not only great at picking guys off first and third; he could pick them off second, too. Sometimes a runner would take liberties at second, but he wouldn't make it too far. Biz would always get him.

Biz was really smart, too. And everybody knew it. He always called the right pitch at the right time. In fact, pitchers rarely shook him off. If they did, he went out to the mound. "I know what I'm doing," he'd say. "Work with me, and I'll get the job done."

He was a good manager, too. When he got that job, we were all very happy. We knew how capable he was. He was a natural leader. And he knew what moves to make—and who should play where. In those days, each team had only 16 or 17 players. A guy might pitch one game and have to play right field the next game. Biz knew how to make those switches and what position each team member should play.

I played under him when he managed the Newark Giants. Originally, I was a shortstop, but Biz moved me to center field. That was a good move. I spent the rest of my career, including my years in the big leagues, as an outfielder—all because Biz was smart enough to see where I should play.

Biz had a lot to do with Roy (Campy) Campanella's career, too. When Campanella was a 15-year-old youngster just starting out with the Baltimore Elite Giants, Mackey took him under his wing and taught him how to catch. For the rest of his life, Campy never stopped crediting Biz for helping him become a Hall of Fame catcher.

Biz was always great to be around. He was a good storyteller. He was jovial, a fun-loving guy. He liked to laugh and tell jokes. When we were on the road, everyone would try to get a seat next to him on the bus, knowing they'd be in for a fun ride. Everyone wanted to sit next to him at dinner, too. People always wanted to socialize with him off the field.

One of the joys of my conversations with him was getting his views on things. I'd ask him about the great players—Louis Santop, Judy Johnson, Satchel Paige, Buck Leonard, and all the others—how good they were and how he would rate them. He'd tell stories about these guys that I could listen to all day.

I was fortunate to know Mackey during the later years of his career. He was always a pleasure to be around, and I will never forget those experiences, how much I learned from him, and how much he contributed to the grand career in baseball that I was so lucky to have.

I am so pleased that Rich Westcott, a distinguished author and uniquely qualified baseball writer, took the initiative to write this book about Biz. He has done a superb job of telling the story of this great Negro League player.

This study is unique in its depth. Going well beyond mere numbers, it delves into the life and career of Biz Mackey—a man who had a major impact on the game of baseball, both in the United States and abroad, and who finally received the well-deserved and long-overdue honor of being elected into the Baseball Hall of Fame in Cooperstown, New York, in 2006.

Baseball fans everywhere will enjoy reading this very special book about an extraordinary baseball legend. Biz Mackey was not only a great player and manager but also a great person. He was Negro League baseball at its best.

—Monte Irvin

Monte Irvin *was elected to the Baseball Hall of Fame in Cooperstown, New York, in 1973. One of the greatest players in Negro League history, he played for 10 seasons with the Newark Eagles,* *between 1937 and 1948 (spending three seasons in the military), during which Mackey was his manager for six seasons. Irvin, who was a baseball and football star at Lincoln University, was one of the first African American players in Major League Baseball. Playing with the New York Giants from 1949 to 1955 and with the Chicago Cubs in 1956, he compiled a career batting average of .293. From 1968 to 1984, he served under Commissioner Bowie Kuhn as the first African American Major League Baseball executive. Sadly, Irvin passed away in 2016, before he could see this Foreword in print.*

FOREWORD BY RAY C. MACKEY III

• • •

I t has been my privilege to work with Rich Westcott, a greatly
admired baseball scholar and author with a deep passion for
Negro League baseball and the shared goal of honoring the
impact of Negro League players on the sport of baseball, U.S.
culture, and people around the globe. I am extremely grateful
to the National Baseball Hall of Fame and Museum and to all
the historians and other members of the special committee that
chose to connect baseball's past to baseball's present, revital-
izing the decades of commitment, hopes, and dreams that my
great-uncle James Raleigh (Biz) Mackey gave to both the game
and the fans who loved him so much.

Never in the wildest of my dreams could I have imagined that
on March 27, 2006, I would receive a call from Cooperstown,
New York, announcing that my great-uncle had been elected
into the Baseball Hall of Fame and that I would be honored
with the privilege of accepting his award in front of millions of

baseball fans. For that and much more, I am forever grateful to the man the world has come to know as Biz Mackey.

Born at the end of the baby boomer years, with a father who was born during the pre-Depression era, I counted baseball as an important part of my youth; it was a favorite pastime for the Mackey family. Growing up, we were avid Houston Astros fans, and, come hail or high water, my dad would ensure that we never missed a season opener. In fact, my father, hospitalized in 1992, passed away on the day of the Astros season opener.

I grew up listening to longtime baseball sports announcer Gene Elston broadcast games over the radio, never imagining that we would share the same stage at the 2006 Hall of Fame induction ceremony, when Elston received the National Baseball Hall of Fame Ford Frick Award. I also grew up hearing all the wonderful stories of my dad's boyhood experiences with my great-uncle Biz, my great-uncle Ernest, and my grandfather Ray Sr., who all played the great game of baseball. But the one thing that fascinated me most about my great-uncle Biz's life in baseball was that during Jim Crow and long before the Civil Rights Movement, here was a Negro man—whose grandparents were born during the time of slavery, from less than meager beginnings—who was traveling the world and enjoying unprecedented experiences. He visited such places as Cuba, Puerto Rico, the Philippines, and Mexico, and he made recurring trips to Japan, where he had the privilege of meeting Emperor Hirohito and, later, the woman who would become the love of his life.

When he was stateside, baseball would take him from Prairie Lea to Philadelphia, from Houston to Hawaii, and to other great places across our nation. It was a lesson to me that a black man from Texas was experiencing such a robust life during this time period. It told me that, in spite of racial color barriers, bigotry, and other discriminatory factors, the game of baseball would usher in goodwill and racial tolerance. Baseball players from around the world, including white Major Leaguers, and fans alike wanted the best players to compete, allowing baseball to serve as a bridge to unity and as a blessing to talented but less-privileged players.

Another contributing factor I had to consider was the great character of Biz and the legacy of the Mackey family patriarchs and matriarchs, who never complained about racial issues or dwelled on the atrocities of the past. Instead, they impressed upon their children and grandchildren that the "burdens of the past" were "mere blessings for the future." They instilled in them the conviction that "all things are possible!" I share with the entire Mackey clan enduring gratitude to Biz for his extraordinary character in setting his sights on a dream and never lifting his eyes from it and for his tenacity in ruling baseball diamonds all over the world.

It is my hope for youth today and for generations to come that, most of all, they glean from the life of the "Giant behind the Plate" the belief he exemplified: that despite humble personal beginnings or imperfect team innings, "all things are possible." For those who read this book and who consider playing this awesome game, I hope that you *catch the baseball buzz with BIZ!*

—Ray C. Mackey III, Great-nephew

ACKNOWLEDGMENTS

• • •

It's never easy to write a book about a subject who no longer exists. Especially one who hasn't been around for more than half a century.

Thus, resurrecting the life of Biz Mackey and his surroundings has been an extremely difficult task. And I could not have accomplished it without the help of many people.

I am especially grateful to Ray Mackey, great-nephew of Biz, who originally presented me with the idea of pursuing this project. Ray's knowledge of Biz's life, his help, and his encouragement were three of the key components in the writing of this book.

I am also grateful to Negro League historian Larry Lester, whose photographs and other contributions, including the compilation of Mackey's game-by-game career statistics assembled with help from his fellow Negro League Researchers and Authors Group member Dick Clark, have been indispensable.

I thank Courtney Smith, whose master's thesis at Lehigh University, titled "A Faded Memory," provided scores of pages of important information about black baseball in the Philadelphia area. And I must certainly salute writer and historian Bob Luke not only for launching this difficult project but also for his help along the way.

Hall of Famer Monte Irvin, who wrote his Foreword and gave me an invaluable interview before he passed away in 2016, also deserves my sincere gratitude. In addition, I am indebted to Dan Stephenson, the Philadelphia Phillies director of video production, who filmed a 90-minute documentary on the Philadelphia Stars that included interviews with five former members of the team.

Baseball Hall of Fame head librarian Matt Rottenberg was extremely helpful with research involving the organization's archives. Additionally, Rob Fitts and Japanese baseball writers Yoichi Nagata and Kyoko Yoshida furnished otherwise inaccessible information about Negro League baseball in Japan. I thank former Phillies player and future Hall of Famer Ryan Howard for his interesting comments.

Others to whom I offer my sincere thanks include Brian Bosley, John Bossong, Kit Crissey, Andrew Ferrett, Donald Hunt, Joe Mitchell, Carl Smith, Bob Warrington, Bob Whiting, Dave Wiggins, and Brenda Wright-Galloway—all of whom provided essential help and information.

Last but certainly not least, I thank my dear wife, Lois, for being here whenever I needed her during this tremendously difficult project. Her help, support, encouragement, interest, and patience are what got me through it all.

In closing, I must say that despite the hardships and the many contradictions and inaccuracies that the study of Negro League history presents, writing this book was certainly an interesting and enjoyable project. Having previously interviewed a number of former Negro League players, I found it fascinating to dig into the history that preceded them and that led to their noteworthy careers.

I thank you one and all for your invaluable help.

BIZ MACKEY,
A GIANT BEHIND THE PLATE

◆ ◆ ◆

INTRODUCTION

The long and formidable history of professional baseball is not one that can be easily digested. In its century and a half of existence, it has had many different components and permutations, many of which cannot be lumped together.

The game, of course, has always been one of hit, run, throw, catch, and think. But that's as far as the continuity goes. There have been changes and differences virtually every step of the way, and that's part of what has made the game so interesting.

Of these various configurations, one that played a significant role in the life of professional baseball was Negro League baseball. From its origin in the late 1800s to its demise in the 1950s, that part of the game made a major mark on the history of the sport.

There are many reasons for this. For much of black baseball's existence, it gave African American players the opportunity to perform professionally in a sport that allowed them no other place to play as pros. In turn, those players' chance to demonstrate their skills proved to be a very special part of baseball history, not only at the professional level but at amateur levels, too.

Although a few African American players did appear in otherwise white big-league baseball in the late 1800s, African American players were barred from playing in the majors for half a century thereafter. During this period of extended segregation, black baseball became highly popular among not only the fans who almost never watched white players perform but also the athletes, who seldom had any other place to play. Most other sports were generally not willing to accept any players other than white players and an occasional Native American player.

Great players and great teams appeared throughout the life of the Negro Leagues. Although theirs is a complex story that is sometimes uncertain due to disagreements among today's historians, and the subjects are often difficult to research due to the lack of available information, Negro League baseball is a fascinating subject filled with intriguing and unusual topics.

One of the most interesting figures in this history was James Raleigh (Biz) Mackey. As his place in the Baseball Hall of Fame suggests, he ranks among the top players ever to perform in Negro League baseball, and he enjoyed a career that was as good as it was long.

Satchel Paige, Judy Johnson, Josh Gibson, Buck Leonard, Oscar Charleston, and Cool Papa Bell are among the greats of the Negro Leagues who have been inducted into the Baseball Hall of Fame. Biz Mackey is part of that group. These great players, all the way up to the Negro Leaguers who became the first African American stars to enter Major League Baseball—Jackie Robinson, Roy Campanella, Monte Irvin, Larry Doby, and Don

Newcombe—played an important part in the history of black baseball.

They played a major role in the careers of some of today's African American big leaguers, too, not the least of whom is Ryan Howard. During a brilliant 11-year career with the Philadelphia Phillies, Howard became the greatest first baseman in the team's 133-year history and its second-leading home-run hitter of all time.

As a youngster growing up in St. Louis, Missouri, Howard learned about the Negro Leagues, he told me. What did they mean to the former National League Most Valuable Player?

"They always made a big impression on me," he said. "My mom told me about them when I was a little kid. Later, I learned a lot about Negro League baseball on my own. The league and its great players were very meaningful. They were a real inspiration to me. Why? Because those were the guys who helped to pave the way for me playing the game and eventually being in the big leagues. I pay homage to them every time I go to one of their events."

Howard's tribute to Negro League baseball certainly emphasizes its importance to the sport and to the players that would follow, both past and present. One of the most important figures during the long era of black baseball was Mackey.

It is generally acknowledged that Mackey was the greatest all-around catcher in Negro League history. Gibson was a better hitter, but Mackey was an outstanding hitter, too, and he could run, field, throw, handle pitchers, and run a game better than any other catcher who ever played in the Negro Leagues.

Even though he never played Major League Baseball, Mackey is considered one of the greatest catchers of all time, ranking at the top with Bill Dickey, Mickey Cochrane, Yogi Berra, Johnny Bench, and Campanella, who as a teenager was taught how to catch by Mackey. Biz's skills behind the plate were as highly regarded as the talents of any of those all-time greats.

Mackey played professionally from 1920 until making his last at-bat in 1947 at the age of 50. According to black baseball historians Dick Clark and Larry Lester (1994), who spent 10 years compiling game-by-game statistics of Negro League players, his lifetime batting average was .327.

Biz spent the best years of his playing career in Philadelphia, including six with the Hilldale Daisies and later three with the Philadelphia Stars, both of which he led to Negro League championships. In those days, Philadelphia was one of the major cities in Negro League baseball; games, including some played at Baker Bowl and Shibe Park, were big attractions, not only to black fans but often to white fans as well. Today, a historical marker stands at the spot where the Hilldale team's home field was in Yeadon, Pennsylvania, and a colorful exhibition celebrating the Stars can be seen near their ballpark in West Philadelphia.

Mackey also played in Indianapolis, Washington, Baltimore, and Newark, collecting large numbers of followers in each place. During his remarkable career, he also managed in parts or all of nine seasons with Baltimore and Newark, winning a championship with the Newark Eagles in 1946. In addition to playing in various other countries around the world, he participated in three exhibition tours to Japan, where he was a highly popular performer and is often credited with helping to elevate the country's interest in baseball.

Truly, Mackey, who came out of Texas as the son of sharecroppers, had a glittering career, and as people throughout this book suggest, it was one highly befitting a friendly person who was liked by virtually everyone he met.

It has been a special pleasure writing this book. That task hasn't been easy, due to the limited and sometimes conflicting information available on Negro League baseball and especially the trips to Japan. Fortunately, numerous books have been written that provide extremely important coverage of the Negro Leagues. I have to say, I learned a lot about not only one of baseball's super catchers but also Negro League baseball in general.

When I was a young boy, my father told me a little bit about it. I learned more as the careers of former Negro Leaguers blossomed in Major League Baseball, especially that of Campanella. Then one of the defining moments came when I attended the Philadelphia Phillies spring training camp in Clearwater the year that John Kennedy became the first African American to appear in a Phillies game (though he wasn't the first black player to be signed by the Phillies: see Chapter 3). I still have strong memories of Kennedy, who was living with a family in a segregated section of town, driving to the ballpark in a dilapidated 1950 Ford.

Later, while covering the Phillies, I got to know Dick Allen, who I hope will become a Hall of Famer, as well as many other African American players, including Garry Maddox, Gary Matthews, Milt Thompson, and most recently Howard and Jimmy Rollins. Among other African American Major League Baseball players, I have interviewed and written in-depth profiles on Irvin, Doby, Lou Brock, Billy Williams, Bob Veale, John Roseboro, and Bill Bruton. The latter had an interesting background story because he was the son-in-law of Negro League all-star third baseman Judy Johnson, who was also Mackey's teammate and a Baseball Hall of Famer. In his later years Bruton lived in Wilmington, Delaware, in Johnson's former house, which was a fun place to visit.

Over the years, I've also interviewed former Stars such as Bill (Ready) Cash, Stanley Glenn, Mahlon Duckett, and Harold Gould. It has always been an interesting experience talking to them about Negro League baseball.

Accordingly, it has been a very enjoyable project researching and writing about Biz Mackey. There are not many biographies written specifically about Negro League greats. But I'm extremely glad that this has now become one of them.

Biz Mackey is regarded as the greatest all-around catcher in Negro League history. (Biz Mackey Foundation.)

• • •

1
. . .

ONE OF BASEBALL'S
GREATEST CATCHERS

Of all the positions on a baseball diamond, none is more demanding or harder to play than catcher. The job behind the plate is without question the most difficult to perform, and those who excel at it rank among the toughest players in the game.

To catch effectively, one has to be a good fielder, have a good throwing arm, be able to call the right pitches, be a good psychologist when it comes to dealing with pitchers, know how to engage tactfully with umpires, how to stave off injuries, and have the fortitude to block the plate and to stand in front of speeding or sliding runners and risk serious injury.

Catching is not a position for the dumb or the lazy or the faint-hearted. To wear the mask and glove, players have to be smart. They have to be tough, fearless, and strong. They must be alert, agile, and accountable. They are the ones in charge of their teams when on the field, and they have to be able to handle that job skillfully.

There are many other qualities required of a good catcher that, put together, determine whether or not players can satisfactorily occupy the position. If they can't, they will not be behind the plate for long.

Rare is the good team that ever took the field without a good catcher. And yet, while baseball has been richly endowed with talented backstops, only a few have ever made it to the top of their profession.

Indeed, of all the 246 players inducted into the Baseball Hall of Fame in Cooperstown, there is only one position—third base—represented by fewer players. As of 2017, there have been only 18 catchers and 16 third basemen elected to the baseball shrine. The reason there are so few catchers is obvious. Typically, in the case of catchers, the Hall inducts those who can both hit and field. Most catchers can play defense well, but few are good hitters, too. So the number of inductees is low.

James Raleigh (Biz) Mackey was a catcher who played both offense and defense superbly. And his place rests securely among the best at Cooperstown.

When the great catchers of the game are discussed, the names first mentioned usually include Bill Dickey, Mickey Cochrane, Yogi Berra, Roy Campanella, and Johnny Bench. These players are known for their vast all-around abilities as hitters, fielders, and leaders on the field. But that group also includes Biz Mackey, even though he never played in the same surroundings as the others.

"You really got paid for your defense," said former Los Angeles Dodgers catcher John Roseboro, who learned much about his position from his teammate Campanella, a native Philadelphian. "Early in my career, I was told, 'Kid, you're paid to get behind the plate and catch the ball, keep the runner from scoring, and throw him out at second. Any offense you give is a plus," he once told the author.

Echoing that sentiment, Dickey, the New York Yankees' great backstop of the 1920s and 1930s, once exclaimed in an interview with the author: "I loved to make a great defensive play. I'd rather do that than hit a home run."

Born in Eagle Pass, Texas, in 1897, before baseball became popular in that area of the country, Mackey developed all the qualities identified with being a great catcher. Although he spent his entire career playing Negro League baseball, it is not stretching the truth to rank him with the great backstops from Major League Baseball as well as to name him the greatest all-around catcher in Negro League history. Even the great Ty Cobb, who was not known for his racial tolerance, once told a now-unknown source that Mackey ranked among baseball's all-time best.

"I couldn't carry his glove or bat," said Campanella, who was originally a member of the Baltimore Elite Giants before he became one of the first African Americans to play integrated Major League Baseball and had a Hall of Fame career with the Brooklyn Dodgers in which he was named Most Valuable Player three times.

As a young player, Campanella learned the art of catching from Mackey. "When I was a kid in Philadelphia," he said, "I saw both Mackey and Cochrane in their primes. For real catching skills, I didn't think that Cochrane was the master of defense that Mackey was."

Ironically, Cochrane and Mackey both played much of their careers in Philadelphia, with the former leading his team to three American League pennants and two World Series championships in three years, between 1929 and 1931. But the predominantly white baseball fan base was largely unaware of Biz's spectacular ability, directing most of its plaudits to the Philadelphia Athletics' backstop.

Mackey is one of three catchers who spent their whole careers in the Negro Leagues and have been inducted into the Hall of Fame. The others are Josh Gibson and Louis Santop. Gibson, an awesome power hitter who led his league in home runs nearly every season throughout a 17-year career that was eventually cut short when he suffered a stroke at the age of 35, is a unanimous choice as the best batter of the three and probably the best power hitter in Negro League history. But Mackey is in a class by himself when it comes to overall ability.

In his book *Josh Gibson—A Life in the Negro Leagues*, William Brashler (1978) writes, "Biz Mackey of the Baltimore Elite Giants was the pro Josh looked to as a catcher when he broke in in 1930. No man in Negro baseball surpassed his ability to handle the position."

"For combined hitting, thinking, throwing, and physical endowment," Homestead Grays owner Cumberland (Cum) Posey once said, "there has never been another like Biz Mackey." Posey—whose catcher with the Grays was Gibson—noted that Mackey was also a "fierce competitor." Mackey, not Gibson, Posey said, "was the best all-around catcher in black baseball history."

In the same vein, Hall of Famer Cool Papa Bell once told Bob Broeg of the *St. Louis Post-Dispatch*: "As much as I admired Campanella as a catcher and Gibson as a hitter, I believe Biz Mackey was the best all-around catcher I ever saw. Gibson was certainly the most consistent power hitter, but he wasn't that good on defense. If I had both him and Campy on the same team, I'd put Roy behind the plate and Josh at first base." Once, Mackey threw out the lightning-quick Bell four times in one game.

In 1952, the *Pittsburgh Courier* took a poll among former Negro League players and sports writers in which it ranked the top Negro League players of all time. The *Courier*, which often took polls among its readers, was one of the leading African American newspapers in the country and, with Pittsburgh being the home of the legendary Homestead Grays and the Pittsburgh Crawfords, was published in what had been one of the nation's leading areas for Negro League baseball.

Along with players such as Jackie Robinson, Satchel Paige, Buck Leonard, Oscar Charleston, and Monte Irvin—all future Hall of Famers—both Gibson and Mackey won spots as Negro League baseball's greatest catchers, with 23 votes going to Josh and Biz getting 15. Some disagreed with this ranking. "He [Mackey] was the best receiver I ever saw," said Leonard, who played with Gibson with the Grays.

The great Judy Johnson, another contemporary of Mackey's and also a teammate on both the Hilldale Daisies and Philadelphia Stars, often talked about the man he seemingly regarded as his brother. "He was the best catcher I ever saw," said the Hall of Fame third baseman from Wilmington, Delaware. "When he played for the Hilldale Daisies, he was the one responsible for their success. I also liked Santop, but felt that Biz was the better catcher."

Some records say he caught in as many as 1,876 games—a figure that would rank him seventh among Hall of Fame catchers. Mackey played professionally in 28 seasons, performing from

1920 to 1947, most notably with the Indianapolis ABCs, Hilldale, and the Stars. Mackey was a key member of both the Daisies' and Stars' only championship teams.

He was still playing at the age of 50, having also served for all or parts of nine seasons as manager of the Baltimore Elite Giants and Newark Eagles. But by then, he was mainly focused on being a teacher and a leader, and he played in only 26 games in his final three years in professional baseball.

Although Negro League records are incomplete and often inaccurate, a detailed study by historians Dick Clark and Larry Lester (1994) determined that Mackey had a lifetime batting average of .327. He played in six All-Star games and was one of the Negro Leagues' all-time leaders, with 702 RBI. In 3,326 Negro League at-bats, Mackey lashed more than 1,087 hits, with 68 home runs. Some other studies say that he posted a .353 batting average against Major League Baseball teams.

While he was obviously not a home run hitter (he hit two home runs in one game only three times and never hit more than seven in one Negro League season), Mackey had four hits in one game 16 times. In 1922, he had five hits in one game three times.

The six-foot-two Mackey, who weighed in the neighborhood of 220 pounds—but who sometimes came to spring training weighing as much as 250 pounds after some heavy off-season eating (it was said that he "never met a calorie he didn't like")—was a switch-hitter who usually batted third or fourth in his teams' lineups and was regarded as a dangerous hitter from both sides of the plate. Few catchers have ever batted that high in the lineup and even fewer have ever been switch-hitters.

Mackey was considered a slow base runner: in his later years, infielder Lenny Pearson, a teammate of Mackey's in Newark, said he "couldn't run a lick." He was once called "a tortoise on the basepaths." Yet he was an excellent bunter, described by Baltimore Black Sox pitcher Frank Sykes as "one of the best bunters the league ever had."

At the plate, though, Biz was regarded as an extremely dangerous, clutch hitter who seldom hit under .300 until his career started to decline in the late 1930s. Mackey won the first Eastern Colored League batting championship in 1923. The Clark and Lester study lists Mackey with a .415 batting average in 1921 with Indianapolis and a .408 mark in 1923 with Hilldale. Once, he was given a base on balls four straight times by Satchel Paige.

Although Paige's walks call into question the full validity of the statement, Biz's former teammate and opponent Johnson once recalled that Mackey would "sting the ball, but pitchers didn't fear him. They wouldn't walk him to get to somebody else."

Irvin recalled that Mackey "was not a power-hitter"; in 1925, he hit his career high of seven home runs. "But he was a very good hitter, mostly a singles and doubles hitter. He hit line drives, and he could hit to any field."

Mahlon Duckett, who played with the Philadelphia Stars when Mackey was an opposing player-manager, labeled Biz "a terrific ballplayer who was just about as good as anybody in Major League Baseball. He was a great receiver and could hit the ball. What more could you ask of a catcher?"

It was on defense that Mackey won the loudest acclaim. Partly because of his spectacular throwing and fielding ability, he played every position, including pitcher, during his career. In both his early days and later years, he was often positioned at shortstop, first base, or right field, playing those positions in 90 games. But when Mackey became a full-time catcher with Hilldale in 1924, it soon became obvious that his defensive skills were unmatchable.

As a backstop, Mackey was easily the best defensive catcher in Negro League history. He was known for his powerful and deadly accurate arm with a quick release and lightning-fast throws. "You didn't have to move your glove six inches off the ground," said third baseman Johnson.

In addition to his ability to catch balls, no matter where they were, with what were often described as "meat-hook hands," Mackey was also known for his unmatched success at throwing out batters who bunted, his agility, his expert handling of pitchers, his thorough knowledge of the game and the strengths and weaknesses of opposing hitters, and his tremendous stamina. Often, Mackey would station himself at shortstop while his team had batting practice, then go behind the plate when the game started. It didn't matter how many innings were played or how hot or cold the weather was: Mackey caught the whole game.

In 1955, Buck O'Neil, a Negro Leaguer in baseball's Hall of Fame and a scout with the Kansas City Royals, put together a retrospective report in order to highlight great players overlooked by Major League Baseball now that teams in "organized baseball" were paying attention to Negro League players. Evaluating players such as catcher Santop and outfielders Willard Brown and Turkey Stearnes, O'Neil characterized Mackey late in his career as being "cat quick defensively." The report added that Biz possessed "good hands [and] a strong arm with quick release and could really control a pitching staff." He was also "quick with the bat, and a good base-runner." He would have been a "very desirable" player to have on the roster.

Pitchers were said to be thrilled to be on the mound when Mackey was behind the plate. That attitude was fueled by Mackey's talent at "framing" pitches, a tool of the catching trade that was and is often used to convince umpires to call a ball a strike. Biz could also catch virtually every foul ball hit anywhere near him. He never yanked off his mask when catching one. And he was aggressive.

"You have to be an intimidator," Roseboro told the author. "You have to be aggressive . . . to be a good catcher."

"As a catcher, he did everything a pitcher needed," said former Philadelphia Stars hurler Harold Gould. "He was a great leader. And you had such a comfortable feeling out there when you were pitching to him. He also had what I think was the greatest throwing arm of all time among Major Leaguers, Negro Leaguers, and every other league."

Mackey loved to snap the ball to first in often-successful attempts to pick off a runner. He threw overhand from a squatting position, even to second base, where his incredibly hard, knee-high throws buzzed past pitchers and often arrived at the bag much quicker than would throws from catchers who were standing. Although Mackey sometimes had to wait until the infielder got to the bag before he threw, rare was the runner who stole a base on him. His throws to second, said longtime standout pitcher Bill Foster, "would come by my mound knee high, and [they] stayed there all the way." After catching a slow curve, Mackey would usually even throw out a runner at second.

During his years at Hilldale, Mackey had a routine between innings with Daisies second baseman Frank Warfield. Biz would fire his blazing throws to the keystone sack, and Warfield would catch them and then yell, "Ow. Mackey, you're gonna kill somebody."

In 1925, Hilldale played the Newark Bears of the International League in a three-game exhibition series. The Bears' Snooks Dowd was his league's top base stealer, but Mackey threw him out seven times in seven attempts. In recapping that story, Hilldale shortstop Jake Stephens said: "Of all the catchers, Mackey was the greatest and the smartest. Nobody, nobody could catch like Mackey. Mickey Cochrane couldn't carry his glove."

In John Holway's (1988) book *Blackball Stars*, Daisies and later Stars pitcher Webster McDonald, who spent 21 years playing Negro League baseball and was one of the game's top hurlers for much of that time, said this about Mackey: "As a catcher, he was the best in baseball, bar none. He was an artist behind the plate. He was the master. It was a pleasure to pitch to him. Santop and Gibson could probably outhit him, but I didn't call them catchers. They were boxers as far as I was concerned. They dropped too many balls. They'd take strikes away from pitchers. Mackey could help a pitcher steal a strike with the way he received the ball. He fooled the umpires sometimes."

Campanella told Holway that nobody, not even Gibson, was as good defensively as Mackey. "I think Mackey by far—by far—in technique and in defensive catching could do it all," he said. To this, Ted Page, who played both the infield and the outfield for many Negro League teams, including the Stars, during his 15-year career, added that Mackey "had moves and everything back there. You had to notice him."

Eighteen-year veteran Jesse Hubbard, who was a longtime pitcher and part-time outfielder, told Holway, "Mackey was the greatest player I ever saw. . . . He was the greatest shortstop, the greatest catcher, a great hitter. Any position you'd put him in, he'd be champ if he could stay there for a month or two."

Although Mackey was known as a catcher with "soft hands," his long years behind the plate were conspicuously displayed by his right hand, his throwing hand. According to Brashler's *Josh Gibson* (1978), "It had been broken at least a dozen times in his career. Every finger was at one time mashed, twisted, sprained, or fractured to the point where his fist became a mangled cluster of bumps and knobs. Still, Mackey did the job, and nothing Josh ever did as a catcher cut into Biz's sterling reputation."

Often playing as many as 10 games per week, Mackey was said to be a "fierce competitor." Biz was also noted by his opponents for his highly competitive spirit, positive attitude, jovial manner, frequent giggling, keen sense of humor, and willingness to banter with hitters, in many cases in an attempt to distract them from the job at hand. He was always talking on the bench, too, and could be somewhat pugnacious if the situation arose. "He was always laughing, always jolly, friendly, always full of fun," pitcher Leon Day, who played under Mackey at Newark, told Holway. "Did you ever hear a magpie chattering and jabbering?" an article in the *San Antonio Express-News* once asked. "Well, Mackey is the epitome of jah-beration. There is not a second when he is behind the bat that he is not chattering or jabbering, exhorting his teammates to show 'a little pepah ou' dere.'"

"You'd go up to bat," added Leonard in an interview with Holway (1988), "and he'd say, 'Well, you're hitting .400. Let's see how much you can hit today.' Or he'd say, 'You're standing too close to the plate.' Or, 'What kind of bat are you using?' He'd tell the umpire, 'Look at his bat there. I don't believe his bat's legal.' He'd say, 'How'd you all do last night? Where'd you play? Aren't you tired? Don't you need no rest? Where'd you sleep last night? I know, you all slept on the bus. You mean you rode all last night and you think you're going to win this ball game?'"

Although barely literate early in his career, Biz, who sometimes signed his name J. Raleigh Mackey and other times just Raleigh Mackey, and who Gould claimed always wore a coat and tie off the field and an extra piece of gum behind his cap on the field, was a dedicated student of the game. "He was the smartest of them all," McDonald said.

In his book *Don't Let Anyone Take Your Joy Away*, Philadelphia Stars catcher Stanley Glenn (2006) added: "He was a big jovial guy, he really loved the game and was probably baseball's best catcher. He was never too busy or [too] occupied to talk baseball. And he was a super handler of pitchers and a clutch hitter."

According to James A. Riley (1994) in *The Biographical Encyclopedia of the Negro Baseball Leagues*, Mackey "had a good baseball mind and employed a studious approach to the game. The ballpark was his classroom, and inside baseball was his subject of expertise. He relied on meticulous observation and a retentive memory to match weaknesses of opposing hitters with the strengths of his pitching staffs. An expert handler of pitchers, he also studied people and could direct the temperament of his hurlers as well as he did their repertoires."

"The way he handled you, the way he just got you built up, believing in yourself, he was marvelous," said pitcher Hilton Smith in "Artist in a Face Mask," Holway's (1988) chapter on Mackey. "I've pitched to some great catchers, but my goodness, that Mackey was to my idea the best one I pitched to. He had hitters looking like they didn't know what to do."

"He was sharp of eye, pugnacious of spirit, and enormous in the clutch," added Ric Roberts, a writer for the *Pittsburgh Courier*. "No better handler of pitchers ever lived."

All of that, of course, was what Mackey always considered to be a major part of the job. In fact, that attitude may have had something to do with how he got his nickname.

There is no certain explanation of how Biz became Biz. One theory is that he was noted as a "busybody." Two more probable explanations are that Mackey was widely known as someone who was especially adept at "taking care of business" or who usually "gave batters the business." Whatever the reason, "Biz" became Mackey's nickname early in his career, and it stayed with him the rest of his life.

Despite all the accolades that Mackey accumulated, there was also a less laudable side to him. He was a heavy drinker and often partied all night, showing up at the ballpark at 10:00 A.M. to shower and then go out to the diamond for some practice. "He often played drunk," Stephens once said, "with his eyes rolling around in his head. But it didn't affect his fielding or his hitting."

Nevertheless, Duckett, who was the last surviving member of the Philadelphia Stars, described Mackey as "a very, very nice gentleman. He was well-liked by everybody."

Mackey also had the habit of arguing with umpires, often to the embarrassment of his teammates. Johnson recalled that in those instances, he would call time and walk over to Mackey, striking up a conversation about girls in order to distract him.

On occasion, Biz also exhibited unusual behavior at the plate. Once, for instance, during a 1928 game against the Lincoln Giants, his bat flew out of his hands while he was swinging at a pitch that was at least a foot off the plate. Highly irritated, Mackey called time, walked over to a patch of grass and pulled up a piece of turf, then put it back in the ground and walked back to the batter's box. On the next pitch, Biz clubbed a single to right field. The grass, he said, helped him get the hit.

During his 28-year career as a Negro League player, Mackey performed in a wide variety of circumstances. He caught most of the great Negro League pitchers, including Paige, who Mackey said threw such a hard fastball that "it could pound steak into hamburger."

Along with the Negro Leagues, Mackey also played against white major- and minor- league teams and toured in California, Cuba, Japan, the Philippines, and Hawaii. Traveling to Japan three times, in 1927 and the 1930s, Mackey and his teammates were said to have played a major role in building the county's interest in the game of baseball, exciting the fans and even Emperor Hirohito, who quickly became a big fan of Biz's.

Mackey performed in four of the first six Negro League All-Star games and on three championship teams, including one that won the Colored World Series. Even in the late 1930s, by which time he had become a player-manager, Mackey was still regarded as the best all-around catcher in the Negro Leagues.

As manager, he helped to send players such as Irvin, Larry Doby, and Don Newcombe to Major League Baseball and won the Negro League championship with the Newark Eagles in 1946. It was as manager of the Eagles that he had his last at-bat in 1947, at the age of 50.

As a catcher, Mackey handled every facet of the job with great skill.
(Negro Leagues Baseball Museum.)

In a fitting climax to Mackey's brilliant career, 100 percent of the baseball and Negro League historians who voted in the *Philadelphia Courier*'s poll said that he should be in the Baseball Hall of Fame at Cooperstown. In 2006, that endorsement came to fruition when Mackey was awarded a long-overdue induction into the baseball shrine.

This is the farmhouse in Luling, Texas, where Mackey lived as a youth. (Biz Mackey Foundation.)

◆ ◆ ◆

2

· · ·

FROM THE FARM
TO THE DIAMOND

In Biz Mackey's early years, no one would've guessed what the future held for him. Baseball was a long way off in the distant future, and present-day survival was the focus of his concentration.

Biz was born James Raleigh Mackey on a date usually listed as July 27, 1897, on a family farm in Eagle Pass, Texas: a town on the Rio Grande River and the first African American settlement in the state.

The town, founded in 1850, had become a temporary outpost for the Texas Militia, which was charged with stopping illegal trade with Mexico. Eventually, the U.S. Army set up a permanent fort near Eagle Pass, and the town was designated as a county seat. Over the years, the fort served as an outpost for U.S. troops fighting off hostile Apaches and during the Mexican-American War, the Civil War, and World War I. It functioned in various capacities, first as a Confederate camp and later, during Mackey's childhood, as a training site for U.S. troops.

Mackey, who was then called Raleigh, was raised on a farm in a nearby town by his parents, Dee and Beulah. Raleigh's grandparents had lived during the era of slavery prior to the Civil War. His parents chose not to burden their boys with stories about the atrocities of slavery, instead focusing on the future and the belief that all things were possible.

Dee and Beulah, whose maiden name was Wright, worked first as tenant farmers until they were bequeathed a portion of land on a local cotton field, which allowed them to become sharecroppers on a small farm of several acres.

James Raleigh Mackey, later called Rollie, had two older brothers, Ray and Ernest, and a cousin, Ophelia, who lived with the family. The Mackeys occupied a four-room house not far from San Antonio—just north of Luling and west of Lockhart.

Amid this land of unbearable heat, dry dust, sagebrush, and wild animals, Mackey and his brothers spent their youth working the farm on the family property. Although they grew up from extremely humble beginnings in a highly uncomfortable rural area, the Mackeys set aside the prejudices and racial barriers of the day and lived a wholesome family life.

They worked hard all day to grow enough food to sell for an income and ate not only the produce they grew but also roosters that they raised on the property. Hot meals, lots of laughter, creating their own fun, and playing sports were at the center of the family's life. Biz's mother, known as Momma Beulah, was a deeply religious, God-fearing woman who made sure her boys understood and knew the God of their forefathers.

The Mackey boys also benefited from their parents' friendship with the Martin family, the original white landowners of the Mackey farm. From that relationship, the boys learned not

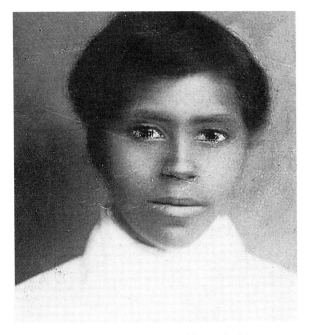

Mackey's mother was known as Momma Beulah.
(Biz Mackey Foundation.)

only that racial prejudice could be overcome but also to respect authority and gain knowledge from other people.

They also gained at an early age a slight ability to read and write. The Mackey brothers attended a grammar school run by the Antioch Baptist Church in nearby Prairie Lea, Texas, where the family worshiped on Sundays. Eventually, the boys graduated from high school, passing what was known as a Common Exam.

Farming, though, consumed a considerable amount of the boys' time, and when they weren't in school, they were required to work with their father through many long hours of the day. Ironically, working on a farm and growing up eating everyday foods such as corn, potatoes, rice, and beans resulted in Biz's becoming a lover of foreign delights later in life. Although as a youth he had never dreamed of playing baseball in places such as Cuba, Mexico, the Philippines, or Japan, when he finally did visit those countries many years later, he developed a special taste for their native meals.

"The summer sun, brilliant and unrelenting, baked the cotton fields between Luling and Prairie Lea," wrote David King of the *San Antonio Express-News* in 2006, when Mackey was inducted unto the Baseball Hall of Fame. "Morning dews quickly turned into thick humidity. The air, stifled by the heat, barely moved, and the weeds clung stubbornly to the red soil. As the summers wore on, the only things more stubborn than the weeds were the cotton bolls, clinging to the scratchy plants on Ernest [Dee] and Beulah Mackey's little farm."

"For countless hours on those beastly days in the early years of the 20th century," King continued, "the couple's boys worked the rows—with hoes early in the growing season and then with burlap sacks at picking time. For a time, they all worked together in those fields, their lives filled with the rhythms of hoeing, picking, hauling, loading, and repeating. It wasn't easy, by any stretch, and it was the kind of hard work that could wear down man, woman, or child."

All along, though, the boys had one major distraction that exceeded all others. It was called baseball. From the time they were young kids, and from the minute they finished working until it got too dark to see the ball, they spent their waking hours playing baseball. Often, Biz would stay to play by himself, once even falling asleep on the field, causing his family to come looking for him in the fear that he'd be bitten by a snake. They'd play anywhere they could find some open space. And with other African American youths as well as some adults from the town, they would play highly competitive amateur games that often drew the attention of local residents.

It is sometimes said that Raleigh was born into a family of baseball players. He began playing the game with his brothers as a young boy. Ray was two years older than Biz, and Ernest was 10 years older. But as boys, they were basically inseparable. They played with makeshift balls and bats. Although his brothers were older, Biz kept up with them, and with his eagerness to succeed at any task, he was always near or above their level of play.

Unfortunately, Dee Mackey passed away when Biz was seven years old. That increased the brothers' responsibilities on the farm, but they still managed to find time to play baseball. And the more they played, the more the Mackeys developed their strength and skill.

Biz also enjoyed foot races with his brothers and friends, and although he wasn't the fastest in the group, he was highly competitive and tried to be a strong runner who could outthink or outwit the others. In that regard, one of Biz's later idols was Olympic champion runner Jesse Owens. Often, Mackey would joke that he wished he had Owens's speed.

Biz hunted, fished, and swam with neighborhood friends. He also had a pet mule who he called "Black Mule." When asked why he liked the mule so much, Biz would jokingly reply that Black could work faster and longer than his two brothers put together. Biz also enjoyed being with the other livestock on the family farm and sometimes would even eat the same food as they did.

Ultimately, Biz stood out from the rest of his baseball-playing group, and the game took over his life. His natural talent was apparent with both the bat and the glove. A switch-hitter even back in those early days, he could hit with distinction from either side of the plate. Moreover, he was a nimble catcher with quick feet and a powerful arm whose strength, it was said, developed in his youth. After all, he tilled the land during planting and harvest seasons; he lifted and hauled the food grown on the farm and loaded hay, watermelons, lumber, and other heavy products onto the horse wagons. Because of that arm, he was often asked to pitch or play shortstop, but he regularly turned down such invitations so he could maintain his favorite position behind the plate.

When Mackey was 18, he and his brothers joined a local Prairie League semipro team called the Luling Oilers. No bunch of weaklings, the Oilers quickly pushed Mackey, who was younger than the others on the team, up the path toward baseball stardom. In 1918, he joined a team owned by a white restaurant owner in Waco, a club that played in the Texas Negro League.

By then, Mackey's mother, Beulah, had remarried. She would, however, pass away prior to Biz's becoming a Negro League star, and after she died, the brothers sold the family farm and split the proceeds. The Mackey parents were both buried in a family cemetery plot near their farm in rural Caldwell County.

Meanwhile, Mackey had a special love for the African American crowds that came to watch him play. He was also excited to notice that white spectators began to attend games to see him and his team. All the while, he possessed a fun-loving attitude toward life, and had a smile when encountering people that he liked, which these crowds appreciated.

Soon, however, the restaurant owner experienced some financial setbacks and sold the team, which was then moved to San Antonio, where it became known as the Black Aces. The team played as a professional team in the Texas Colored League, a thriving league made up of teams from various parts of the state. Even then, Mackey thought that someday, sometime, he might break the color barrier and play Major League Baseball.

The Black Aces, taking the field with six players who would later perform at the highest Negro League levels, shared a white team's ballpark, but quickly became the favorites of the local populace. Drawing crowds as large as 3,500, and attracting big newspaper coverage, the Aces sent Mackey to the mound on numerous occasions. As a hard-throwing pitcher with an underhand curve ball, Mackey not only distinguished himself on the mound but also hit well over .300 while playing shortstop and catcher.

After finishing the season in first place in 1919 with a 45–10 record, the Aces met the team from Dallas in the league championship game with Johnny (Steel Arm) Davis starting on the mound for San Antonio. In the first inning, Davis gave up two runs, and with one out, Mackey was summoned to the mound. Biz got out of the inning unscathed, but he gave up a lone run in the third inning and two in the fifth.

The Aces came back with five runs in the sixth to tie the score, which included a bases-loaded single by Mackey. Then, in the eighth, Mackey's RBI single drove in what accounted for the winning run. Biz retired the side in the ninth to give the Aces the championship.

After the game, the *San Antonio Express-News* had special praise for Mackey, calling him the "one player from the team who has come the closest to baseball immortality."

A young Mackey broke into pro ball with
the San Antonio Black Aces. (NoirTech Research, Inc.)

The following season, the Black Aces' owner, Charlie Bell-
inger, sold the rights for Mackey and six other players to his friend
C. I. Taylor, a prominent black businessman and owner of the Indianapolis ABCs. About that time—and for reasons unknown—
Beulah and her second husband separated, sometime prior to
1920.

Climbing up the ladder to professional baseball was always
Biz Mackey's main ambition. And it happened rather quickly.

The ABCs were a highly reputable team, and without giving it a second thought, Mackey signed with them and moved to Indianapolis. The ABCs, so named because their founder in the early part of the 20th century was the American Brewing Company, were originally an independent team. But in 1920, they became one of the charter teams in the newly formed Negro National League, joining seven other teams, including the Kansas City Monarchs, the Chicago American Giants, the Detroit Stars, and the Cuban Stars. The ABCs quickly established themselves as one of the elite teams in the circuit.

Along the way, in addition to Mackey, the ABCs would sign other young talent, such as future Hall of Famer Oscar Charleston, pitcher Dick (Cannonball) Redding, Dizzy Dismukes, Ben Taylor, Crush Holloway, and various others, thereby forming one of the league's strongest teams.

Twenty-two years old when the 1920 season began, Mackey spent his first year in Indianapolis playing shortstop, third base, and right field; pitching; and occasionally catching. For the season, he hit .289 with seven home runs, and the ABCs finished fourth with a 39–35 record.

The following season, Mackey established himself as one of the ABCs' best players. He hit .415, again with seven home runs. In one game, he went 4-for-8. Meanwhile, in the field, Biz was playing mostly second and third base, while Indianapolis was posting a 35–38 record and a fifth-place finish.

It was then that Biz got his first taste of the rest of the country. Traveling during that season, the ABCs made stops in Darby to play the Hilldale Daisies, in Ebbetts Field in Brooklyn, in Atlantic City, and in Richmond, Virginia.

That winter, Mackey and a team of Negro Leaguers traveled to the West Coast, where they played in the California Winter League, a circuit that included players from the Pacific Coast League and Negro League stars. During the season, Mackey was credited with a .382 batting average. Afterward, the team, known as the Philadelphia Royal Giants, won seven out of 11 games in an exhibition series with a Major League Baseball team led by brothers Bob and Irish Meusel. Mackey was said to have hit .341 in that series.

Mackey's career changed in 1922, when he spent most of the year as a catcher. He still played a few games at shortstop, third base, and right field, but his main position was catcher, and that launched what would become a Hall of Fame career.

Mackey hit .382 that year with eight home runs. The ABCs registered a 46–33 record, while finishing in second place. Unfortunately, serious internal problems surfaced, Taylor died, and the team fell into poor financial shape. That condition would worsen, and after the 1925 season, the ABCs went out of business, although a team with the same name would return to Negro League baseball in 1931 and play through 1938.

But by 1923, Biz decided he'd had enough. He signed a contract and, with teammate Ben Taylor, jumped to the Hilldale Daisies of the new Eastern Colored League. Playing with the Daisies, one of the league's best teams, would raise Mackey's status to an even higher level.

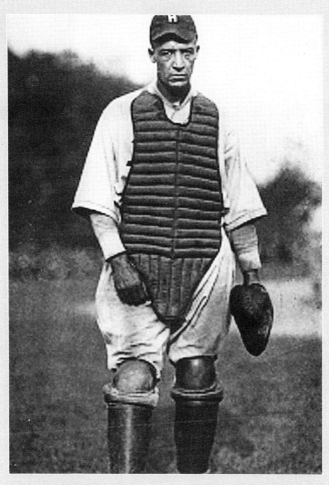

Louis Santop was a future Hall of Famer who played in Philadelphia with Hilldale. (Biz Mackey Foundation.)

◆ ◆ ◆

3

• • •

BLACK BASEBALL
IN PHILADELPHIA

There was a time many years ago when Philadelphia was regarded as one of the top areas in the country for black baseball. As a player for two of the city's greatest black teams, Biz Mackey had a major role in earning that designation.

Although a form of baseball played by white players has been traced back to the early 19th century, African American baseball in Philadelphia went back a long way, too, beginning in the 1860s, when the first black teams were formed. It continued through the first half of the 20th century, when Philadelphia was at various times the home of some of the most prominent teams and players in the Negro Leagues.

Philadelphia, of course, was noted for many special achievements in sports, and not just in baseball, although it was where the first National League game was played in 1876. The University of Pennsylvania fielded its first football team in Philadelphia in 1876. The nation's first college basketball game was played there in 1895, when Haverford College defeated Temple University, 6–4. That same year, Philadelphia was the site of the first Penn Relays and the first Devon Horse Show. In 1899, the first Army-Navy game was played in the city.

Black baseball also had a rich tradition in the city and played a major role in these early years of local sports. During more than eight decades of black baseball, the city was the home of the Pythian Club, the Excelsiors, and later prominent professional teams such as the Philadelphia Giants, Hilldale Daisies, and Philadelphia Stars. At various times, scores of amateur black teams thrived throughout the region, too.

Players were eager to perform for Philadelphia professional teams. The pay was decent, off-season jobs were always available, one could find satisfactory housing, and racism was far less pronounced than it was in many other areas of the country. It helped that the city's large African American population (by 1920, Philadelphia's black population of 134,000 was the second-largest in the country) strongly supported black baseball.

Some of the most highly decorated players, such as Hall of Famers Judy Johnson, Oscar Charleston, Rube Foster, Martin Dihigo, John Henry (Pop) Lloyd, and Satchel Paige, competed on Philadelphia teams. Among the 17 Negro Leaguers who entered the Baseball Hall of Fame in Cooperstown in 2006, seven inductees—players Biz Mackey, Frank Grant, Pete Hill, Louis Santop, King Solomon (Sol) White, and Jud Wilson, as well as team owner Effa Manley (a native of Philadelphia)—had Philadelphia connections.

So, of course, did Hall of Famers Roy Campanella and Reggie Jackson. Campanella was a Nicetown native who first played Negro League ball before becoming a three-time Most Valuable Player with the Brooklyn Dodgers and the second African

Future Hall of Famer Judy Johnson also
played in Philadelphia during the early part of his career.
(Urban Archives, Temple University.)

American (after Jackie Robinson) elected to the Baseball Hall
of Fame. Jackson, from Wyncote and a graduate of Cheltenham
High School, had a total of 563 home runs and won four home
run titles during his storied 21-year career. Playing mostly with
the Oakland Athletics, New York Yankees, and Cleveland Indians, he helped win five World Series titles.

A version of baseball—much different from today's game—
was originally played in Philadelphia by white teams as far back

as the late 1700s. By 1830, a game that was known mostly as "town ball" and sometimes "cat ball" was on its way to becoming a highly popular sport. A few college baseball teams were formed in the 1850s, and by 1860 hundreds of club teams populated the area. Ultimately, a team called the Athletics was formed in 1865. The squad fielded one of the first paid players, a left-handed second baseman from England named Al Reach, who later became the owner of a prominent sporting-goods company and, in 1883, the first owner and president of the Philadelphia Phillies.

Meanwhile, African American baseball teams first surfaced in Philadelphia during the Civil War, when black soldiers in the Union army, as well as freed slaves, played the game. The game was a source of pride among African Americans, and by the late 1860s, there were numerous black club teams in the city, most notably the Excelsiors (formed in 1866), the Pythians, the Orions, and the Keystone Athletics, all highly skilled teams made up mostly of players from the Philadelphia area. In fact, black baseball in the city was prominent as early as 1867, when the Excelsiors traveled to Long Island for a meeting billed as a "championship" game.

That same year, the Pythians, a club for young black men that met once a month at a rented meeting hall at 718 Lombard Street, formed a baseball team. The Pythians soon became especially noteworthy, not only because of their success on the field but also because of their leader. Octavius V. Catto, a former army officer and a teacher and later principal at the Institute for Colored Youth (which later became Cheyney University) at 715 Lombard Street, helped to organize the Pythians and then became their promoter, manager, and second baseman. Included in Catto's aspirations was his devotion to the growing attempt to end segregation in the United States.

The Pythians won their first two games by scores of 35–16 and 62–7. Soon afterward, they tried to join the all-white National Association of Base Ball Players and then another group called the Pennsylvania State Convention of Base Ball Players, both leagues of teams scattered throughout Pennsylvania. In both cases, however, the applications were rejected by the group's board, which voted to ban any team "composed of one or more colored persons." Ultimately, the team played other newly formed black clubs, once winning a game with a 52–25 score and another 50–43. The team played most of its games either in South Philadelphia or Camden.

Under Catto, the Pythians became the first black baseball team to face an all-white club. On September 3, 1869, they played the Olympic Club, a prominent white team, at the Olympic Grounds at 25th and Jefferson Streets in North Philadelphia. (In 1876, the field, by then known as Jefferson Park, was the site of the first National League game, when the Athletics beat the Boston Red Caps, 6–5, reportedly before a crowd of 3,000.)

With their largest crowd to date, an integrated collection of spectators numbering an estimated 5,000, Olympic defeated the Pythians, 44–23. The game was said to be played in two hours and 50 minutes, and there were no incidents among the orderly fans, who cheered fervently for their teams.

A few weeks later, the Pythians met another all-white team, called the City Items (sponsored by one of Philadelphia's daily newspapers). Playing at Columbia Park at 15th Street and Columbia Avenue, the Pythians won this time, 27–17.

The game, of course, was not then played with the same rules that it has today. There was no pitching mound, and hurlers were positioned 45 feet from home plate. A batter could call for a low or a high pitch, and if he struck out, he would still become a base runner unless the catcher threw him out at first. Also, a ball was ruled fair if it bounced into fair territory anywhere on the field.

In that era of black baseball, the Pythians, who often lured away the better players from other teams, played home games at 11th and Wharton Streets and occasionally at Recreation Park—later the first home of the Phillies—at 24th Street and Ridge Avenue. Over time, they increasingly played white teams and out-of-town teams and often moved to other areas themselves to play a game.

Games were often social affairs, followed by dances and picnics. Male fans brought food and cigars not only for themselves and the home team but also to share with the opposing team's players. The postgame activities were the climax of these nights, which brought neighboring communities together and fostered close friendships between them.

The pinnacle of the Pythians' success came in 1869, when they defeated the Uniques, a powerful black team from Chicago, in what was called the World Colored Championship. Two years later, the 32-year-old Catto, also a prominent civil rights activist who worked tirelessly for the integration of the city's streetcars and for the passage of the 15th Amendment, which allowed black men to vote, was murdered by a white segregationist as he walked to his home on South Street in South Philadelphia. Catto's death, an enormous tragedy that affected the entire city, was followed by a funeral cortege that at the time was the largest for a black man in Philadelphia history.

Catto's death sent the Pythians into a downward spiral. They floundered miserably, and within a few years they dissolved. African American baseball in Philadelphia, however, continued to flourish, and as the 19th century progressed, the Olympic Club became the dominant team in the area and black professional teams had begun to form.

By the 1880s and early 1890s, more than one dozen players—including the widely known Moses (Fleetwood) Walker—had played in white professional leagues. (Walker is credited as the first black athlete to play Major League Baseball, performing with the Toledo Blue Stockings of the American Association in 1884.) Although such integration didn't last long, black pro baseball teams were starting to form, with teams in Harrisburg, Trenton, York, Millville, and Williamsport. In 1887, the first black league, called the Colored Baseball League, was formed, with Philadelphia fielding one of the six teams. The league folded after one month because of disagreements between the teams.

In 1902, a pro team was organized by Walter (Slick) Schlichter, the white sports editor of Philadelphia's *The Item*, and Harry Smith, a baseball writer with the black *Philadelphia Tribune* newspaper, who joined with a prominent black player named Sol White to form the Philadelphia Giants. Nicknamed King Solomon, White had been a standout player since 1890 and was one of the most prominent and influential figures in black baseball.

The Giants quickly became one of the leading black teams in the country and, in their first season in 1902, compiled an 81–43–2 record before ending the year with a two-game series against the American League champion Philadelphia Athletics, losing both games. In 1903, bolstered by the addition of stars such as Pete Hill, Grant (Home Run) Johnson, and Charlie

Grant, a light-skinned second baseman who John McGraw of the National League's Baltimore Orioles had once tried to sign by passing him off as a Native American, they lost to the Cuban X Giants in five of seven games in what was billed as the "World's Colored Championship."

The following year the Giants signed a brilliant young pitcher named Andrew (Rube) Foster (so nicknamed because he once defeated Philadelphia Athletics pitching great Rube Waddell), who had beaten the Giants in four of the Cubans' five playoff wins the previous year. This time, though, the Giants beat the Cubans in two out of three games, all played in Atlantic City, with Foster winning both games to win the world title. There was no championship series in 1905, although Foster won 51 of the 55 games in which he pitched.

Along the way, the Giants occasionally played white teams. In 1904, for instance, they met the International League's Newark Bears, then managed by future New York Yankees general manager Ed Barrow. In a four-game series, the Giants won every time. The Giants often played these matchups at Columbia Park, owned by the American League's Philadelphia Athletics, at 29th Street and Columbia Avenue, or at the Phillies' Philadelphia Park (later renamed Baker Bowl), located at Broad Street and Lehigh Avenue.

The Giants paid salaries that ranged from $60 to $90 per month. Led by future Hall of Famer Lloyd, the team claimed to have compiled a record of 426–149 from 1903 through 1905, including a 134–21 mark in 1905.

The team joined the International League of Colored Baseball Clubs in America in 1906. At the time, the league consisted of teams from not only Philadelphia but also Wilmington, Brooklyn, and Riverton/Palmyra (New Jersey), as well as two Cuban touring teams. In addition, the Giants played every Negro club in the East, including ones in Chester and Camden, plus some in the Midwest. On September 30 that year, they played three games in one day—a morning game in Elizabeth, New Jersey, and then afternoon and evening battles in Brooklyn.

That year, en route to a season record of 108–31–6, they clinched the title against the Cuban Giants, winning 5–3 with two runs in the ninth inning in a one-game championship series before 10,000 at Columbia Park. This was the largest crowd ever to attend a series between black teams, and the game was the first to be played by two black teams in a Major League Baseball ballpark.

Soon after the 1906 series ended, Schlichter challenged the Philadelphia Athletics, who in the previous five years, since the American League was formed, had won two pennants. In a two-game series, Eddie Plank and the Athletics won the first game, 5–4, and in the second game, Waddell pitched a two-hit shutout to win, 5–0.

Foster moved on to Chicago in 1907, and in the same year, White left the club following a disagreement with Schlichter. Despite their departures, the Giants entered the championship round in 1908 but lost to Foster's Leland Giants and thereafter won no more titles. Meanwhile, another African American professional team, the Philadelphia Quaker Giants, attracted some fans but lasted only one year. At the end of 1909, two years after White's departure, the Philadelphia Giants dropped out of the league. They played as an independent team until disbanding after the 1917 season.

Black baseball, though, was still very much alive in the Philadelphia area, which by now had become a prime destination for black migrants from the rural South during what was known as the Great Migration. The city's black population numbered some 85,000 in the early 1900s. Typically, those who were baseball fans shunned the white Athletics and Phillies Major League Baseball clubs to watch black teams that played throughout the city and surrounding areas. Amateur and semipro teams in all parts of Philadelphia, as well as in areas such as Germantown, Chester, Norristown, Ardmore, Ambler, Doylestown, Wilmington, and Camden, thrived, drawing large crowds on sandlot fields for not only the baseball games but also the hugely popular social events that often followed.

A team called the Hilldale Daisies (or sometimes the Giants or the Darby Daisies) had been formed in 1910 as an amateur team for young black men from Darby, a town just outside Philadelphia in Delaware County. Hilldale soon became the top team in the region, eventually relocating to a new ballpark in nearby Yeadon where games—mostly against white teams—often attracted crowds numbering 6,000 to 8,000, with many spectators riding packed trolley cars to the ballpark.

The Daisies turned professional in 1917, playing an independent schedule that in 1920 included games against two barnstorming Major League Baseball all-star teams, one featuring Babe Ruth. Then in 1923, Ed Bolden, a post office employee, helped to form and became president of the Eastern Colored League (ECL), which featured top professional teams from throughout the East Coast, including Hilldale.

With Lloyd as the manager and future Hall of Famers Johnson and Santop in the lineup, Hilldale won the league championship in 1923, 1924, and 1925. In 1924, a postseason series was arranged with the Negro National League, another top circuit that operated mostly in the Midwest. In what was called the "Colored World Series," Hilldale lost to the Kansas City Monarchs. The following year, however, the Daisies beat the Monarchs to win the title, triumphing in the final game at Hilldale Field in Yeadon before a crowd estimated at 8,000.

Over the years, other outstanding players such as Mackey, Dihigo, Nip Winters, and Phil Cockrell dotted the Hilldale roster. Johnson, a native of Wilmington, Delaware, was the highest-paid player, earning $130 every two weeks.

As one of the top franchises in the nation, the Daisies were followed by black fans throughout the country. Teams from other areas clamored to play in the city, where exhibition games were booked and promoted by local sports entrepreneur Eddie Gottlieb. "The Mogul," as he became known, was also part owner of a sporting-goods company, and one of its clients was Hilldale. A dusty Hilldale ledger showed that spikes could be purchased for $18 and a baseball glove for between $5 and $6.

By 1920, the black population in Philadelphia exceeded 130,000. Despite this growth, the ECL folded in 1928, and the Daisies drifted back and forth between an independent schedule and membership in two short-lived professional leagues. Then, at the end of 1932, with Bolden having pulled out, new owners in control, and the team drawing poorly as the Great Depression ravaged the economy—it drew just 99 fans in one home game— the team disbanded.

The area's baseball tradition was bolstered by many kinds of teams: a professional team called the Bacharach Giants, which played out of Atlantic City, New Jersey, and lost to the Chicago American Giants in the 1926 World Series; the Philadelphia Tigers, which played in the Eastern Colored League in 1928 and lasted just one year; and more strong sandlot teams throughout the area than there'd ever been. In North Philadelphia, West Philadelphia, and South Philadelphia, and again in Ambler, Ardmore, Camden, Chester, Norristown, and Wilmington, high-caliber African American teams played heavy schedules before large crowds, sometimes competing against teams of white players.

Several independent teams, including the previously pro Bacharach Giants (owned by one of Gottlieb's sporting-goods partners, Harry Passon), the East End Giants of Germantown, and the West Philadelphia Giants, East Philadelphia Giants, and North Philadelphia Giants, all developed large groups of followers in their home areas and often played pro teams. (It was considered standard procedure in those days to name your team the Giants.)

Long before other sports with African American superstars from the Philadelphia area drew attention—stars such as Wilt Chamberlain in basketball; Emlen Tunnell, the first black player elected to the Pro Football Hall of Fame; one-time heavyweight boxing champion Joe Walcott; pro golfer Charley Sifford; and Olympic track star Carl Lewis, among legions of others—baseball was overwhelmingly the favorite sport of black Philadelphians. Enormously popular in each section of the city where teams operated, the sport virtually controlled the social and economic lives of the local residents and served as a way for them to communicate with each other and, at least temporarily, to escape the ugly racism and other struggles that often assailed them.

Philadelphia's status as a major center of black baseball was enhanced in 1932 with the formation of a new professional team called the Philadelphia Stars. After starting as an independent team, often playing clubs such as the Monarchs and the Pittsburgh Crawfords at Shibe Park and Baker Bowl, the Stars joined the newly reformed Negro National League (NNL) in 1933.

With Gottlieb—who later became a leading figure in pro basketball as one of the founders of the National Basketball Association (initially called the Basketball Association of America) and the first coach and eventual owner of the Philadelphia Warriors—serving as the principal owner and with Bolden running the team, the Stars captured the NNL title, beating the Chicago American Giants in a seven-game series. Again, Mackey was one of the mainstays of the team, along with pitchers Slim Jones and Webster McDonald and infielders Dick Lundy and Jud Wilson.

The Stars never won another league crown. But, originally playing home games mostly at Parkside Field at 44th Street and Parkside Avenue in West Philadelphia, they performed respectably throughout the 1930s and early 1940s with players such as Charleston, Turkey Stearnes, and Gene Benson leading the way. Even hurler Satchel Paige played briefly with the Stars.

Along the way, the Phillies were embroiled in a stunning event. Having lost 100 or more games in five straight years and having finished in the first division only once (1932) since 1917, the Phillies had gone bankrupt and been taken over by the National League. The League sought a new owner, and in 1942 Gottlieb, along with two well-known local friends, brothers Leon and Isaac Levy, attempted to buy the team. Reportedly, they were rejected by National League president Ford Frick because they were Jewish.

Among the other candidates was Bill Veeck, whose father owned the Chicago Cubs. Although it was never recorded elsewhere and the story has been disputed, Veeck, who became one of baseball's great promoters, claimed in his book *Veeck as in*

Wreck that he made an offer to purchase the Phillies in 1943. He said that once he became owner, he planned to stock the roster with Negro League stars.

Veeck's idea was reportedly vetoed by Frick and Judge Kenesaw M. Landis, who was then the league commissioner. The denial of this deal meant that black players lost their best chance of breaking the color barrier at that point in Major League Baseball.

A few years after Veeck's attempt to buy the Phillies, Jackie Robinson became the first African American in the 20th century to play Major League Baseball, when he joined the Brooklyn Dodgers in 1947. Robinson's first game in Philadelphia was a history-making event in which 41,660 (40,952 paid) came to Shibe Park to watch the Dodgers and the Phillies play. With fans arriving as early as 5:00 A.M. for an afternoon doubleheader, the jam-packed stadium, stuffed with more than 5,000 over capacity, played host to the largest crowd in the ballpark's 62-year history. Also for the first time in the ballpark's history, a large number of African Americans attended the game, and they cheered loudly each time Robinson came to bat.

Soon afterward, other black players, including Campanella, signed contracts with Major League Baseball teams. Veeck went on to own the Cleveland Indians, where he brought in Larry Doby in mid-1947 as the first African American to play in the American League. Veeck later was the owner of the St. Louis Browns.

Among the other black players who entered the big leagues were Monte Irvin and Don Newcombe. Both played on teams managed by Mackey, as did Doby. That was good for the players and the campaign to end segregation in Major League Baseball, but it also virtually assured the end of Negro League baseball.

The Stars continued to play, but their attendance dropped precipitously as an increasing number of players moved into "organized baseball," taking many fans with them. Like all black teams, the Stars sold players to big-league teams, including outfielder Ted Washington to the Phillies in 1952. Drafted during the Korean War, Washington, a native of Camden, New Jersey, never played in the Phillies system because of injuries suffered in battle. But his signing did argue against the myth that for many years haunted the Phillies, that the club's racist configuration prevented it from signing black players in the early years of baseball's integration. Included in that view was the fact that Campanella had unsuccessfully asked the Phillies several times for a tryout.

Ultimately, infielder Chuck Randall, a football and baseball standout from Glassboro High School in New Jersey, was signed by the Phillies in 1955 and became the first African American to wear a Phillies uniform, donning the red and blue attire in spring training the following season. Then in 1957, infielder John Kennedy became the first African American to appear in a Phillies game, playing in five of them that year.

Pitcher Bob Trice in 1953 became the first black player signed by the Philadelphia Athletics, although various reports over the years suggested that Connie Mack had an interest in signing black players, including Mackey, long before this actually happened. In fact, according to Robert Peterson's (1970) book *Only the Ball Was White*, Mack wanted to sign both Mackey and Santop in the late 1920s but was vehemently discouraged from doing so by other team owners. Mack, who in the 1950s would hire Judy Johnson as a scout, was said to have continued to pursue black players, but again was unsuccessful in those attempts and backed away from his interest in African American players until Robinson broke the color barrier.

The 1952 season was the last one for the Stars. The team was shut down at the end of the season, and despite later attempts to revive them, the Stars were gone for good. With them went more than 80 years of African American baseball in Philadelphia.

Philadelphia, however, continued to hold a prominent place in the annals of black baseball.

In 1969, for instance, the Phillies captured the headlines when they traded Dick Allen, Cookie Rojas, and Jerry Johnson to the St. Louis Cardinals for Curt Flood, Tim McCarver, Joe Hoerner, and Byron Browne. Flood, an African American and a 12-year veteran, refused to report to the Phillies. Instead, he filed a suit against Major League Baseball, contesting the reserve clause, which gave teams the right to determine where and for whom a player performed. The case advanced all the way to the U.S. Supreme Court, which ruled against Flood. But the point had been made. Soon afterward, the reserve clause was eliminated by Major League Baseball, and a whole new approach to contracts was started. Because of Flood's desire not to play for the Phillies, baseball was never the same again.

Over the years, though, numerous players have come out of the Philadelphia area to star in Major League Baseball. In addition to Campanella and Jackson, the list includes Overbrook High School's Jeff Leonard, a star outfielder with the San Francisco Giants and several other teams who was named the National League Rookie of the Year in 1979; outfielder Pat Kelly, out of Simon Gratz High, who had a standout 15-year career in the American League; and Philadelphia-born Dion James, an 11-year big-league outfielder.

The Phillies over the years have fielded an impressive group of African American players to stand beside these native sons in the ranks of Major League Baseball. Among them have been star performers such as Allen, Dave Cash, Garry Maddox, Bake McBride, Gary Matthews, Milt Thompson, Marlon Anderson, Jimmy Rollins, and Ryan Howard. All have helped to make Philadelphia arguably the top city in the country in the annals of black baseball history.

Mackey was still playing in the field,
mostly at shortstop, when he started out with Hilldale.
(Biz Mackey Foundation.)

◆ ◆ ◆

4

• • •

BLOSSOMING WITH
THE DAISIES

In the annals of Philadelphia black baseball, no team rates higher than the Hilldale Daisies. The Daisies (or Giants, as they were sometimes called) were not only the area's all-time leader on the field; they were also an enormously popular squad that usually packed the stands when they played.

The Daisies were one of more than 100 black baseball teams that dotted the Philadelphia landscape during the more than 80-year period of segregated baseball. For 20 years, the team played most of its home games at a well-manicured field known as Hilldale Park, located at Chester and Cedar Avenues in Yeadon on the edge of Delaware County. Huge crowds would stuff the park to watch the Daisies play once they became a professional team. A Pennsylvania Historical Society marker now honors the site of the old ballpark.

The Daisies, so named because daisies grew every spring in right field at Hilldale Park, originated in 1910 when a 19-year-old from Darby, named Austin Dever Thompson, sought other

African American youths living in the area to join a team. As a team created for black teenage boys from Darby, a town with a large African American population in Delaware County that bordered on Southwest Philadelphia, the Daisies played in their early years as an amateur squad. The squad was put together and managed by Thompson, but he left the team before the end of the first season, and 29-year-old Ed Bolden, a Darby resident who worked as a post office clerk in Philadelphia, took over as manager while supplying the team with equipment purchased from Passon Sporting Goods, a business partly owned by sports icon Eddie Gottlieb.

In the ensuing years, the strong-willed Bolden not only recruited players from other teams but also worked fervently to publicize the Daisies in the local papers. "We have good grounds and give a good guarantee for a good attraction," Bolden wrote in the *Philadelphia Tribune*. Bolden even advertised that his club "would like to arrange games with all 14- and 15-year-old traveling teams" and would pay half their expenses.

Hilldale went from an unknown club to one of the best of the many African American teams that were scattered throughout the Philadelphia area. As an amateur and then semipro team, Hilldale always posted wins that far outnumbered its losses and drew crowds that regularly reached at least 3,000. After the Daisies held their own against the professional Cuban Stars and Brooklyn Royal Giants, Bolden decided to recruit top players and incorporate the team, turning it into a professional club in 1917 and registering it as African-American Hilldale Corporation. Bolden named himself president, and the team began signing players and meeting other pro and semipro squads in the area.

At first, the Daisies played an independent schedule against both black and white teams. Soon they were attracting professional players from elsewhere—the team's first pro player was outfielder Otto Briggs, previously of the Indianapolis ABCs—and becoming increasingly prominent. Eventually, the Daisies were playing, with considerable success, against not only teams from Philadelphia, Chester, Camden, Norristown, Ardmore, and Trenton but also teams from other areas.

Negro League baseball had become extremely popular among black sports fans throughout the country, and Hilldale was no exception. Watching the Daisies play at home was always a special occasion. Tickets cost as little as 25 cents. Picnics and dances often followed the games. On each year's opening day and often after weekend games, the game would serve as a social event. "They had bands," recalled Ed Bacon, a local player who once served as the Daisies batboy, in an article by Jim Walker in the Delaware County *Daily Times.* "The women had fried chicken, ham sandwiches; [there were] lots of people outside and blind people with cups."

Veteran catcher Louis Santop, one of the great catchers in baseball history and a future Hall of Famer, joined Hilldale in 1918 for a monthly salary of $450, an astronomical sum for that era. Two years later, Bolden added another future Hall of Famer to the squad—Judy Johnson, then a young infielder from Wilmington—as well as an assortment of other top players, including pitcher Phil Cockrell and shortstop Dick Lundy.

The Daisies posted a 41–7 record in 1918. In one game, they defeated former Major League Baseball pitcher Chief Bender. Over the next few years, they continued to play teams of past and present Major Leaguers. "The race people of Philadelphia and vicinity are proud to proclaim Hilldale the biggest thing in the baseball world, owned, fostered, and controlled by race men," Bolden said in a letter to the *Tribune* in another of his frequent attempts to publicize his team.

Bolden was obsessed with the idea of making Hilldale one of the best teams in professional baseball. He wanted to attract not only the top players but also the top crowds to a stadium that, even many years later, was remembered fondly by those who saw it. "If you stood there the way I did, you'd never forget it," said Carl Smith, who grew up in Yeadon and played youth baseball games at the ballpark. It was just a terrific field even when I played there in the 1940s. It was just one heckuva fine field."

In 1919, the Daisies played the Bacharach Giants from Atlantic City in a game that marked the first time two black teams met at Shibe Park. The following year, Hilldale met in a series of games against a team of big-league all-stars, including Babe Ruth. Playing some of the games at Baker Bowl, home park of the Philadelphia Phillies, the Daisies won just one of five games. But their reputation as a strong black team was now reaching well beyond the East Coast.

Accordingly, in 1921 Hilldale became a member of the Negro National League (NNL). At the end of the season, Hilldale, winner of more than 100 games overall for the first of two straight years, met the American Giants of Chicago, a powerful NNL team, in a six-game series in Philadelphia. With three games played at Baker Bowl and three at Hilldale Park, the Daisies, led by Johnson and Santop, won three, lost two, and tied one.

But Bolden constantly feuded with the American Giants and their NNL leader, former Philadelphia Giants pitcher Rube Foster, a future Hall of Famer who had brought stability to Negro League baseball when he formed the league. Ultimately, after two seasons in the NNL, the ambitious Bolden became so disenchanted with Foster and the NNL that he pulled his team from the league and became the driving force in the formation of the Eastern Colored League (ECL). The new league staged its first games in 1923.

Bolden, who emphasized "clean baseball" and insisted that his team maintain high moral standards—he once issued warrants for the arrest of five fans for their "rowdy" conduct at a game (four of them paid fines, and ultimately Bolden hired security guards for future games)—was more than a little anxious to field the best team in the league. After all, as one who had fiercely battled the rich and the powerful and eventually bailed angrily out of the NNL and put together the new ECL, Bolden prioritized making a good showing.

With that in mind, he quickly set about signing new players. Raiding the NNL as well as independent professional teams, Bolden inked, among others, pitchers Jesse (Nip) Winters and Holsey (Scrip) Lee, shortstop John Henry (Pop) Lloyd, first baseman George (Tank) Carr, and outfielder Clint Thomas. All were established stars, and Lloyd was a future Hall of Famer who often was compared favorably with Pittsburgh Pirates great Honus Wagner.

Bolden also persuaded another young player with the Indianapolis ABCs to join the Daisies. He went by the name of Biz Mackey. Mackey's ultimate arrival in Philadelphia launched a career of nine years spent in the City of Brotherly Love.

Initially, with the aging Santop handling most of the catching duties, Mackey performed for Hilldale mostly at shortstop, where he would replace the much older Lloyd, and sometimes at third base or first base. Bolden, who ran the team but had appointed Frank Warfield as manager, wanted Mackey's bat in the lineup on a daily basis. On days when Santop needed a break, Mackey also went behind the plate. Eventually, Biz would play every position on the diamond with the Daisies, including pitcher.

It didn't take long for Mackey to win the endorsement of Hilldale followers. The 25-year-old Texan quickly showed that he was an excellent hitter and a player who loved the game. The *Tribune* soon proclaimed that "[Mackey] plays the game with all the enthusiasm of a schoolboy." *Pittsburgh Courier* sports writer Rollo Wilson nicknamed the lovable Mackey "Baby Doll."

During his years with Hilldale, Mackey lived in a second-floor apartment over a restaurant in Darby. Mackey always tried to live near restaurants, and when traveling or playing with other teams, he would try to lodge near his favorite places to eat. "It always made it seem like I was home," he said.

Mackey at short and Warfield at second would entertain fans with their antics during infield practice. Mackey would fire the ball to second with his customary speed, and Warfield would scream, "Ow, Mackey, you're gonna kill somebody."

Despite being too big for the position, standing six feet two inches and weighing about 220 pounds, Mackey played shortstop more than any other place in the field. And he played the position well: so well, in fact, that even in his later years as a catcher, it was obvious that he had the tools to play a key infield position.

In his book *Blackball Stars,* John Holway (1988) quoted Jake Stephens, another Hilldale shortstop, as saying, "He didn't have the range I had. But he was a better shortstop than I was. He never threw the ball harder than he had to. When a hard hit ball came to Mackey, he'd take and bounce it down on the ground and throw the man out."

The 1923 Daisies, with Lee, Cockrell, and Winters turning in one sparkling pitching performance after another, proved too much of a match for the rest of the ECL, winning 32 of 49 games and the league championship. Overall, Hilldale is said to have posted a 137–43–6 record during those two seasons.

According to the statistics compiled by Dick Clark and Larry Lester (1994), Mackey, spraying hits all over the field, was credited with winning the league batting championship in 1923 with an average of .415 with four home runs. "He hit line drives from the left side and from the right side he hit with power," said pitcher Chet Brewer. "No right-hander would throw him a curveball or he would get it hit into right field."

Mackey also spent some time at first base, a position that some thought would become his regular spot. "Bizz [sic] Mackey, whose versatility on the diamond is known to the fans everywhere," one newspaper article claimed, "has horned into the limelight recently as a first baseman. The big boy from Texas shows marked agility for his poundage and takes high, wide and difficult throws with the ease of a regular." With Santop and Spunky Joe Lewis doing the catching and Stephens getting a lot of time at shortstop, the article reported, "this leaves Bizz to break in at another point and the way he is slugging the apples, he's too valuable a man to keep out of the game."

Before the 1924 season began, Mackey was offered the chance to jump to the Homestead Grays, one of the leading teams in Negro League baseball. He reportedly accepted owner Cumberland (Cum) Posey's offer, but then walked away, returning to Hilldale. That season, Hilldale, after holding spring training at the downtown Philadelphia YMCA, continued its run as one of the best teams in Negro League baseball. In a game on August 4, Biz went 5-for-5, taking over as team leader while still playing mostly at shortstop following Bolden's release of Lloyd for causing "dissention." With Cockrell, Winters, Lee, and Rube Currie leading a brilliant pitching staff, the Daisies again won the ECL championship, posting a 47–23 league record, which was five and one-half games above the second-place Baltimore Black Sox, and recording a 112–51–9 mark overall.

During the season, Mackey had distinguished himself in an exhibition game with the semipro Farmer's Club of Brooklyn, New York. "Mackey drew rounds of applause from the stands," it was reported, "when he flung himself at full-length on the ground and took Allen's bad throw, hooking his foot across the bag in time to force out the sliding Shannon at second."

His performance in the field, however, was inconsistent. In some games he played spectacularly, and in others his glovework was terrible. Several weeks after his spectacular play against the Farmer's Club, the situation was reversed when Mackey committed four errors in a game against the New York Lincoln Giants. "The big shortstop kicked in with a quartet of glaring miscues that sided materially in the New York team's run-making," a reporter wrote.

This time, though, Hilldale's success extended beyond its triumphs in league and independent ball. With fans and sports writers pushing for a championship series between ECL and NNL winners, the first Colored World Series was scheduled, with the Daisies meeting the famed Kansas City Monarchs in what would turn out to be a 10-game event. The president of the

NNL was Rube Foster, who, because of his dislike for the ECL, had prevented previous series between the two leagues.

The teams split the first two games, both played at the Phillies' Baker Bowl. Kansas City won the opener 6–2. In the second game, Hilldale won 11–0, with Mackey getting two hits and scoring three runs, before a crowd that totaled more than 8,600. In the ensuing battles—with two games played at Baltimore, three at Kansas City, and three at Chicago—the Monarchs emerged with the championship with five wins, four losses, and one tie, that being a 13-inning, 6–6 game called off because of darkness. Mackey was intentionally walked three times in that game. In the first game at Kansas City, Mackey scored on Johnson's three-run homer in the ninth inning to give Hilldale a 5–2 victory. In the sixth game, Mackey singled in the first inning and scored Hilldale's first run on Johnson's triple in a 6–5 Daisies win.

The turning point in the series occurred in the eighth game, when the 35-year-old Santop dropped a ninth-inning foul pop-up off the bat of the Monarchs' Frank Duncan. Four pitches later, Duncan hit a ball through the legs of Mackey, who was playing third base while Johnson had been moved to shortstop, and two runs scored. Although Mackey was not charged with an error, Santop was, and the mishaps led to a 3–2 Kansas City win. After the game, manager Warfield unleashed such a nasty tirade at Santop that it brought the aging catcher to tears. Ultimately, after winning Game Nine, 5–3, with Mackey lacing two hits, the Daisies lost the series with Biz popping out to end the final game, a 5–0 Monarchs win.

In the end, with attendance across the series totaling just under 46,000, the winners received $4,927.32 to divide among them, and the losers had $3,284.88 to split.

Ultimately switching to catcher, Mackey became one of the Daisies' top players. (NoirTech Research, Inc.)

Ultimately, Warfield's outburst paved the way for Mackey to become the team's full-time catcher, with Santop, who had once been described by a local reporter as "a Philadelphia tradition like scrapple and political corruption," relegated to a role as backup catcher and pinch-hitter. Biz, who had the third-best batting average in the league, with .324 with four home runs in 1924, now not only was one of the most dangerous hitters in the league but also was stationed at the position at which he would become one of the best players in all of baseball.

Bolden, by then the team's manager, was roundly lauded for moving Mackey behind the plate. "Receiving, by the grace of Bolden, will be Biz Mackey, an all-around player, but a catcher by nature, and a darned good one at that," one local reporter wrote.

Mackey had his own way of catching. He talked constantly

to batters, with the intention, he said, of "distracting" them. He never pulled off his mask to catch pop-ups. He snapped line-drive throws to second base from a squatting position, getting the throw to the bag quicker and more accurately than most catchers could do standing up.

In time, Mackey's spectacular defensive skills, along with his uncanny ability to call pitches, would earn him a ranking as the greatest defensive catcher in Negro League history. "Nobody could catch like Mackey," Stephens once said. "Mickey Cochrane couldn't carry his glove."

The 1925 season would prove to be the high point in Hilldale's rich history and another great year for Biz. Having spent the previous winter in Cuba, where he posted a .309 batting average for the Almendares team, Mackey returned to Yeadon and hit .349 with a career-high seven home runs. The Daisies, led by Winter's 26–4 mark, registered a 52–15 league record, romping to the ECL title.

Again Hilldale met the Monarchs in the Colored World Series. This time, though, the Daisies prevailed. With the first four games played in Kansas City and the last two at Baker Bowl, Hilldale won five out of six games to capture the crown. The Daisies scored three runs in the 12th inning to take a 5–2 win in the first game, with Rube Currie going the distance. They lost the second game, 5–3, but came back to win Game Three, 3–1, in 10 innings, on RBI hits by Namon Washington and Bill Robinson. Warfield's two-run triple sparked a four-run ninth inning as Hilldale won the fourth game, 7–3. Back at Baker Bowl, Currie's seven-hitter and Mackey's RBI double helped the Daisies win again, 2–1.

This ticket to the 1925 Colored World Series entitled the holder to a seat in the grandstand. (Rich Westcott.)

Hilldale, with Cockrell on the mound, clinched the championship with a 5–2 victory in Game Six at Baker Bowl. Mackey's fifth-inning double off the wall drove in one run. He then scored the final run of the series with what was described as "a terrific blow" over the right-field wall, where balls landed in Broad Street at the risk of hitting passing cars. Mackey wound up hitting .375 in the series.

Afterward, Hilldale players received $69 per man for their efforts. An article in the *Tribune* informed readers that the Daisies, who in later years have often been called one of the great teams in Negro League history, were "one of the most perfect baseball machines with every player working in unison."

The 1925 season turned out to be the last great year for the Daisies. In 1926, Biz, who had become one of the most feared hitters in the league while batting from either side of the plate, hit .335, but Hilldale slipped to a 34–24 record and finished in third place. The best part of the year came after the ECL season, when the Daisies met a team of Major Leaguers that included

American League batting champion Heinie Manush of the Detroit Tigers, Cleveland Indians slugger and MVP George Burns, and Philadelphia Athletics stars Lefty Grove, Rube Walberg, Eddie Rommell, Bing Miller, and Jimmy Dykes. The Daisies won five out of six games, with Winters beating Grove in one game, 6–1, with Mackey getting a key hit.

By 1927, financial problems were beginning to plague Negro League baseball, and, with their salaries cut, many players were thinking about earning their livelihoods elsewhere. Mackey was one of them. By then, rumors, although unfounded, had begun to circulate that Bolden was planning to trade Biz. When the opportunity came for him to become part of a team of black players

The greatest team in Hilldale history was the 1925 club, which won the Colored World Series. (Biz Mackey Foundation.)

The 1925 Hilldale Giants

who were going to barnstorm in Japan, Mackey quickly joined 13 other players to form the first African American team to play in Asia. The team was called the Philadelphia Royal Giants.

The tour conflicted with Negro League baseball's spring training as well as the regular season, causing team owners to claim they would take "drastic action" against any player who joined the tour. "It is unreasonable for players to expect that they could ramble around in the Orient, and then report to their teams," *Tribune* columnist J. M. Moss wrote.

Mackey's departure was reported to "have fallen like a bombshell in the ranks of Hilldale fans," and the league threatened him and the other barnstormers-to-be with five-year suspensions. But Biz and his new teammates departed from California in March anyway. "Players not owners fill the seats at the ballparks," Moss claimed. "Hilldale needs Mackey. The East [ECL] will most likely find some way to wink at the new rules and put Mackey back in good graces."

The Negro League team played in Japan for two months (see Chapter 6). It returned to the United States on May 20, and, shortly afterward, Mackey was seen sitting in the stands during a game at Hilldale Park. Mackey's presence so excited fans and players alike that the Daisies twice defeated the league-leading Bacharach Giants. Soon thereafter, Bolden decreased Biz's suspension to two months. Mackey made his first 1927 appearance in the Daisies lineup on July 24.

Before that, Hilldale had posted a disappointing 17–28 record. But then, clearly demonstrating the value of Mackey in the Daisies lineup, the team registered a 19–17 mark the rest of the way. In one game after his return, Mackey scored twice and drove in three runs with a double and a triple. In another game, he swatted two home runs and a triple while scoring five runs and driving in four more to account for nine of his team's 22 runs. Showing their appreciation for a grand slam he smashed one week later, fans gave Biz $40, a nice bonus for a guy whose monthly salary was $175.

Mackey finished the season with a .318 batting average while pulling Hilldale up to a third-place finish with his second-half performance. After the season, he joined the Homestead Grays for some exhibition games.

By then, however, financial troubles, caused largely by diminishing fan support, were plaguing not only the Daisies but most of the other teams in the league as well. Money problems had become so severe for Hilldale that late in the season Bolden suffered a nervous breakdown and was committed to a mental hospital.

After recovering, Bolden, by then involved in a widening dispute with the other ECL leaders over what he claimed were "selfish motives," withdrew his team from the league. Hilldale became an independent team, playing against both amateur and semipro teams while holding virtually all its games at Hilldale Park so the team could gather the gate receipts.

Mackey, meanwhile, had spent the winter of 1927–1928 in Southern California playing on a black team sponsored by Shell Oil Company. The team played exhibition games, including some against Major Leaguers. With his superior talent, Biz easily attracted the attention of his white opponents, some of whom lamented his exclusion from the big leagues.

In 1928, Mackey returned to the Daisies, who spent much of spring training on a road trip, playing 14 games in southern cities against a team from Schenectady, New York, called Buck

Ewing's All-Stars. That season, Biz hit .349. In an often-told story, he lost his bat while swinging at a pitch. He missed the next pitch by a foot, then called time and walked over to a grassy spot on the field, where he plucked a piece of turf out of the ground. He then replaced it in the ground and returned to the batter's box, whereupon he slammed a line drive to right field for a single. Biz said later that he "relied" on grass to bring him luck.

After the season, Hilldale played three exhibition games against the Athletics, a team on the verge of winning three straight American League pennants and two World Series. In one game Biz got three hits off of Joe Bush, and in another he laced two hits against Ed Rommel. Grove held him hitless in the other game, but the Daisies won two of the three contests.

These games offered a close-up chance to compare the Daisies' catcher with another all-time great catcher playing in Philadelphia at the time. Mickey Cochrane was a future Hall of Famer, like Mackey, who played for 13 years in the big leagues with the Philadelphia Athletics and Detroit Tigers. The consensus was that Cochrane might have been a better hitter, but Mackey had a better arm. Overall, though, said Winters, "I don't know who was better."

The following spring, Mackey once again had a yen for travel. This time, he went to Hawaii, where he played for two months with another touring team of black players that included Hilldale teammates George Carr and Ping Gardner. Bolden claimed he would suspend his absent players one game for each day they were absent. Upon his return, Mackey spent part of that time out of action, but not as much as Bolden had originally planned.

By the time Mackey returned to the diamond on June 24, Bolden had carved out a new route for his team. The Eastern

League had disbanded, and Hilldale had joined the newly formed American Negro League (ANL). But the Daisies, even with future Hall of Famer Oscar Charleston in the lineup, could only finish fourth, despite a 24–15 record in the second half after Mackey came back to the team, which had gone 15–20 in the first half. Biz wound up with a .331 batting average for the season. That fall, he returned to California, where he again played against white Major Leaguers, including Jimmie Foxx, Al Simmons, and Bob Meusel.

With the Great Depression now taking a heavy toll on the nation's economy, Negro League baseball's already weakening financial condition had reached the point of desperation. The ANL was one of the victims, folding after just one season. With no money and little interest in continuing with the sport, Bolden joined the exit by selling the Daisies to John Drew, a wealthy black politician and businessman who owned a transit line that ran from Delaware County to Philadelphia (which he later sold to the Philadelphia Rapid Transit Company).

Hilldale, which Drew renamed the Giants, was once again reduced to independent status for the 1930 season, with games scheduled by Gottlieb, the prominent entrepreneur and local booking agent who was the dominant scheduler of amateur games in Philadelphia. Owner of the basketball team the Philadelphia SPHAS (South Philadelphia Hebrew Association), Gottlieb also sold Hilldale its baseball equipment as part owner of Passon Sporting Goods.

That year, Mackey played briefly with Hilldale, although some of his worthiest teammates, such as Johnson, Charleston, Stephens, and pitcher Webster McDonald, had already departed. At one point, Mackey caught Cockrell's sixth no-hitter of the season.

But eventually, Biz left the Daisies, joining the Baltimore Black Sox for the final month of the season and hitting .408 for the year.

But as the Hilldale team became involved in some intricate financial maneuverings between Bolden and Drew, Mackey returned in 1931 to a new club owned by Bolden and called the Hilldale Daisies. (According to Negro League historian Bob Luke [2011], Drew retained ownership of the original team, called the Hilldale Giants.) With Dihigo now on the roster, as well as McDonald, Johnson, Stephens, Bill Yancey, and Rap Dixon, Mackey hit .344, with Hilldale posting a 42–13 record as an independent club.

It was Mackey's final year with Hilldale. The following spring, he rejoined the Royal Giants and toured Japan, Hawaii, and the Philippines. Biz spent the summer with the Royal Giants, never appearing in a Negro League game the entire season. Meanwhile, Hilldale joined the newly formed East-West League (EWL), but both the league and all its teams struggled throughout the 1932 season. At the end of the season, the Hilldale team was dissolved and its tenure as a top Negro League was forever finished.

Mackey, though, would not be gone from Philadelphia for long. He would soon return, rejoining Bolden and Gottlieb on a brand new Negro League team called the Philadelphia Stars.

Mackey (back row, fourth from right) was one of the leading players
when the Philadelphia Stars won the Negro League championship in 1934.
(NoirTech Research, Inc.)

◆ ◆ ◆

5

• • •

HELPING THE STARS
TO SPARKLE

When the Hilldale Daisies withered and died after the 1932 season, the Philadelphia area was without a high-level African American team for the first time in nearly 30 years. But the void didn't last long.

Just one year later, a new team called the Philadelphia Stars began to make its mark on the local baseball scene. Formed as an independent team in 1933, the Stars moved into the big time in 1934, launching a run that would last for nearly 20 years.

Along the way, the Stars would become one of the city's most popular teams. Its roster was bolstered by local players as well as some of the all-time greats of Negro League baseball, including Biz Mackey.

Although the team began at the height of the Great Depression and the crowds at games were originally small, the Stars had the advantage of taking the field when the city's two Major League Baseball teams ranked low among professional teams. The American League's Athletics had won three pennants and two World Series between 1929 and 1931, but with Connie Mack dumping his star players because, he claimed, he couldn't afford to pay them big salaries, the A's were cascading toward the bottom of the heap, winding up with seven last-place and two seventh-place finishes between 1935 and 1943. Meanwhile, the National League Phillies were in the midst of a 31-year period in which they finished in the first division only once (1932). In the 17 seasons between 1926 and 1942, they wound up in last place 10 times and in seventh place four times.

Within Philadelphia's professional sports landscape, the Stars came out at just the right time. With baseball on the rocks, the Philadelphia Eagles just getting started in 1933, and there being no major-league basketball or ice hockey teams, Philadelphia fans were desperate for a team worth watching. The Stars fulfilled that need, attracting both white and black fans to their games, which were played initially at Hilldale Park and then at Passon Park at 48th and Spruce Streets. They also played Monday night games at Shibe Park.

The team was launched by Ed Bolden, former director of the Hilldale Daisies, who had sold that team in 1930. Bolden solicited the services of Eddie (Gotty) Gottlieb, one of the area's most well-known sports figures.

In addition to his role in the sporting-goods business, Gottlieb was the premier booking agent in the Philadelphia area. His contemporaries knew that a local amateur or semipro team couldn't get a game unless it went through him. For many years, he had also been one of the Negro Leagues' top booking agents, and he often scheduled games at Shibe Park and Yankee Stadium.

He was a co-founder and coach of the Philadelphia SPHAS, which in the 1920s and 1930s was one of the leading pro bas-

ketball teams in the country. In 1946, he would be one of the
founders of the Basketball Association of America (BAA), which
later merged with the National Basketball League to form the
National Basketball Association. In 1946, when the BAA began,
he was also coach of the Philadelphia Warriors and would lead
them to the league's first championship. Six years later, he became the team's owner.

Nicknamed "The Mogul," Gottlieb was a heavy-duty sports
figure. When he was brought in by Bolden to join the Stars, his
principal duties were to provide funding, run the business op-
erations of the team, and serve as a booking agent, scheduling
nonleague games. Bolden was the titular president who took care
of the baseball side of the business, but Gottlieb, who often paid
his players individually in men's restrooms so one player wouldn't
know what another earned, and always watched games from a
seat in the stands, was the primary owner of the team.

Wishing to build a formidable team right from the start, the
Stars' executives went on a recruiting spree, raiding other teams
for good players. One of the first players they signed was Biz
Mackey. Once Hilldale's star catcher, Mackey had played with
the Daisies until 1931 and then in Japan through most of 1932.
Bolden was determined to get him for the Stars and pursued him
relentlessly until he signed.

Mackey was joined on the Stars by leading players such as ace
pitchers Webster McDonald, Phil Cockrell, and Stuart (Slim)
Jones; first baseman Ernest (Jud) Wilson; outfielder Rap Dixon;
infielder Jake Stephens; and shortstop Dick Lundy, the team's
manager. Cockrell, who began his career in 1916, was said to
have pitched more no-hitters than any hurler in black baseball
history.

The Stars played an independent schedule in 1933, facing both black and white teams and drawing crowds of people of all races to their games. They opened the season with a two-game series in York, Pennsylvania. In another game, they defeated the vaunted House of David team, 5–1, with Mackey slugging a key single. Among the teams they played most often were ones from Camden, Frankford, Mayfair, and South Philadelphia. They also played doubleheaders on both Saturdays and Sundays and sometimes during the week.

There was another notable black professional team in the city that competed with the Stars for local popularity—the Bacharach Giants. This team was owned by Gottlieb's former business partner, Harry Passon, who had started the SPHAS along with Gottlieb and Hughie Black and had become a major sporting-goods dealer in the area with Gotty as one of his original partners.

But with Bolden placing advertisements for games in local papers, the Stars took over as the city's most popular black team. They played throughout the city and suburbs, appearing nearly every day of the week. On Sundays, they often played in Camden because of Pennsylvania's Blue Laws, a state curfew that prevented teams from playing sports on that day. In one game, they played the New York Black Yankees at Hilldale Park and drew a rousing crowd of 5,000 fans. They also played an all-white team from the New York–Pennsylvania League. And they regularly indulged their fierce rivalry with the Bacharach team.

Mackey was named captain of the team, and he hit .289 for the season. Also in that 1933 season, he was named the starting catcher in the inaugural East-West All-Star team, beating out a young Josh Gibson, even though the Stars were not yet members of the NNL. Joining Mackey and Gibson on the East team were

Ed Bolden not only was a key figure with the Hilldale Daisies but also was
the originator of the Philadelphia Stars.
(John W. Mosley Photograph Collection, Charles L. Blockson Afro-American Collection,
Temple University Libraries, Philadelphia, PA.)

Judy Johnson, Oscar Charleston, and Lundy, but they lost to the West, led by Turkey Stearnes, Willie Wells, and future Major Leaguer Sam Bankhead, 11–7.

By then, the Stars were facing considerable pressure to join the NNL. Some of the league leaders, especially Cum Posey of the New York Cubans and Gus Greenlee of the Pittsburgh Crawfords, relentlessly pursued Gottlieb in an attempt to get him to bring his team into the league. And in 1934, Gotty did just that. It would turn out to be the most glorious year in Stars history.

The 1934 season was noteworthy for all professional sports in Philadelphia. Because of the fierce advocacy of Gottlieb, Athletics manager/owner Connie Mack, Eagles owner Bert Bell, and Phillies majority owner Gerry Nugent, a state referendum voted to overturn the Blue Laws, which had forced hardships on so many teams. Prior to that, all Philadelphia teams had to schedule Sunday games elsewhere; in the Stars' case, they frequently played doubleheaders in Baltimore against the Black Sox when they weren't in Camden. Although the Blue Laws ended, the city retained a curfew that prevented teams from playing after 7:00 P.M. on Sundays.

That year, the Stars also switched their home games from Passon Field to a new diamond at 44th Street and Parkside Avenue in West Philadelphia, just off of Belmont Avenue and near the famous Sesquicentennial building in Fairmount Park. Called Penmar Park, it was an attractive baseball park that could hold up to 8,000 spectators.

On Sundays, crowds that could reach more than 10,000 spectators, many of them standing, would jam into the park. Men wearing coats and ties and women decked out in dresses, gloves, hats, and high-heeled shoes sat cozily in the stands watching a team that had considerable appeal to the local fans.

The Stars, with Mackey hitting .315 for the season, were extremely successful, so much so that sports writer Randy Dixon of the *Philadelphia Tribune* saluted the "honorable" Bolden for placing a baseball team "on local green pastures that should well merit the approval of the most critical fandom." Later, after the Stars had defeated the NNL's formidable Pittsburgh Crawfords in an exhibition game, Dixon wrote that the club "had stepped in the front rank of eastern Negro baseball."

There was, however, one problem with Penmar Park. Built in the 1920s by the Pennsylvania Railroad for use by that company's team, it was placed alongside a railroad track. Trains would leave the nearby roundhouse, traveling along the tracks. Cinders, sparks, and soot would fall on the field and stands, and dense smoke would billow out of the engines. People were sometimes burned. And the smoke would frequently surround the baseball field, causing fly balls to be lost and games to be delayed for as much as 15 minutes.

"Every time we played," said Mahlon Duckett, an infielder who played with the Stars from 1940 to 1949, "we would have to stop the game until the smoke cleared from a passing train." Duckett added that the club often wore dark travel uniforms to hide the grime and dirt from the locomotives.

With McDonald now managing the team in place of the released Lundy, who now piloted the Newark Dodgers, the Stars opened their first season in the NNL on May 13, against the Dodgers. The Octavius V. Catto Elks Band led both teams to a flagpole for the national anthem, then commissioner Rollo Wilson, a former sports writer and Temple University graduate, threw out the first ball. The Stars won the game, and their new place in black baseball was underway.

The Stars posted a 12–9 record in the first half of the season, finishing second behind the Chicago American Giants. They then romped to an 11–4 mark in the second half to finish first and ended the league season with a 23–13 mark. During the second half, the Stars and three other black teams had played some exhibition games at Yankee Stadium against other NNL teams to benefit two slain police officers. An interracial crowd of more than 30,000 attended the event. The Stars also played a five-game series against the Bacharach Bees, as they were now called, in what was billed as the City Championship. The Stars won in five games.

Sports writer Ed Harris of the *Philadelphia Tribune* said that the Stars had used the help of star players to present black baseball as "fit for the big-time leagues." He added that this disproved the notion that "Negro baseball isn't worth a dime."

When the season ended, the Stars had the second-best overall record in the league. That qualified them for a battle in the championship series with Chicago, owners of a 28–15 league record. Led by future Hall of Famers shortstop Wells and outfielder Stearnes, plus other outstanding players, such as pitcher/catcher Ted (Double Duty) Radcliffe and first baseman George (Mule) Suttles, the American Giants had, with the exception of a few years, been one of the top teams in the league since the NNL was formed in 1920.

Although league historians have presented several different versions of the series, the most likely is this: in a seven-game series, the Giants won the first game, played in Philadelphia. Then, moving to Chicago, McDonald pitched the Stars to victory. The fifth game was marked by controversy after two Stars players had physically attacked an umpire but were not ejected. Ultimately, the Giants had a three-games-to-two lead when a fight on the field among players from both teams and a subsequent contentious battle with league commissioner Wilson resulted in a 10-day delay.

Afterward, the Stars won the sixth game, 4–1, to even the series. Then the seventh game at Penmar Park was stopped when it reached curfew time, with the score tied at 4–4.

Jones was supposed to pitch the eighth game, but McDonald wasn't sure, even though Jones said he felt good and was ready to pitch. "Pitch Slim, Mac. Pitch Slim," Mackey pleaded. Biz got his wish, and it turned out that the catcher knew what he was saying. In the game, again filled with contentious play, Mackey singled home a run in the fourth inning to break a 0–0 tie. Then Jones slammed an RBI double to give the Stars a 2–0 victory and the championship.

In their first year in the league, 1934, the Stars were the champions. Mackey, who missed part of the season because of an injury, hit .315 with two home runs during the season, while batting .368 in the championship series. Wilson led the team in batting, with a .364 average, while Jones, who had become a standout pitcher with the help of Mackey, had an overall mark of 20–4 with a 1.24 earned run average in 203 innings pitched. Overall, the Stars, with players earning an average salary of $350 per month, had a 50–26–4 record, including nonleague play.

Although Mackey was 36 years old, his all-around skills were more highly regarded than the long-ball slugging ability of Gibson, who was just starting to knock on the door of stardom. In fact, Mackey's defensive game was so much better than that of all other catchers in black baseball that he was chosen for four of the first six all-star games and two more later on. "He did a wonderful job behind the plate, mopping up four runners," one newspaper reported after a game during that 1934 championship season.

Obviously, Mackey had captured the attention of the local fans and the press with his spectacular catching exploits. The *Philadelphia Tribune* said that Mackey was "known the length of the country for his uncanny throwing arm and destructive batting." The statement was no exaggeration.

"He's the best catcher in baseball, bar none," McDonald said. Of course, McDonald was an outstanding player, too. Once when he was pitching and Mackey was catching in an exhibition game, the batter, Jimmie Foxx, yelled at Mackey: "Have him throw me something I can hit and don't throw me that bender."

Ernie Jones, the father of former Philadelphia high school, college, and professional basketball star Wali Jones and a skilled baseball player in his younger days, spoke in 2016 about his first-hand experience watching Mackey compete. At 100 years of age, Jones told how he and his friends used to sneak into Passon Field to watch the Stars play. "We were only 15 or 16 years old," he said, "but you could see he was a great catcher. He was one of the greatest catchers who ever lived. Maybe not as good of a hitter as Josh Gibson, but certainly a great catcher."

In addition to his defensive skills, Mackey had the ability to take the young pitcher Slim Jones under his wing and turn him into one of the best hurlers in the league. Jones, who ran up a 13–1 record in his first year, in 1934, was often called a left-handed Satchel Paige. Along with mentoring Jones, Mackey also brought out the best in Nip Winters, and between the two pitchers, he would develop two of the best left-handed hurlers in black baseball history.

At one point, Jones was regarded as the fastest pitcher in base-ball, surpassing such hurlers as Paige and the Athletics' Lefty Grove. But his fate after his baseball career illustrates the differ-ence between the lives of retired professional athletes then and now. Unfortunately, one winter several years later, Jones—now with a bad arm, out of money, and suffering from a drinking problem—sold his overcoat so he could buy a bottle of whiskey. Soon afterward, he died frozen on the street in Philadelphia.

The 1934 season would be the last big moment for the Stars. Never again would they be in a championship playoff, despite playing for another 18 years.

Following the end of the season, the Stars played a barnstorm-ing team comprising brothers Dizzy and Daffy Dean, Paige, and other professional players. Headed by the Deans, who had just led the St. Louis Cardinals to a World Series win over the Detroit Tigers, this team met the Stars in a doubleheader before a large crowd at Shibe Park. McDonald pitched the Stars to an 8–0 win in the first game. The second game was called because of dark-ness after seven innings. In the two games, Mackey, who played first base, slugged three hits and drove in three runs.

Afterward, Mackey and some of his fellow players, including Frank Duncan, Newt Allen, Chet Brewer, and Bullet Joe Rogan, accepted another invitation to play in Japan. This time they also played in China, the Philippines, and Hawaii. They arrived home in time for the 1935 season, which saw the Stars sink to a 28–27 overall record, while Mackey hit just .252. Despite their inability to reach their previous lofty heights, the Stars played on. Mackey was still the team's captain and star player. Most of the time, he played catcher. But once in a while he played in the outfield or at first base.

Around that time, he met a 13-year-old boy who was often seen hanging out at the ballpark. Mackey gave him a few pointers and discovered he had a knack for teaching. A few years later he became a full-time mentor who taught Roy Campanella the rudiments of catching (see Chapter 8).

The 1935 season proved to be Mackey's last in Philadelphia. During the winter, Bolden, who was ill through some of the season, traded him to the Washington Elite Giants. Mackey not only hit .291 for the season; he also served as interim manager for three weeks during the campaign.

Mackey would serve as a player-manager for much of his remaining career, which ended in 1947. Meanwhile, the Stars remained a part of the NNL, but with nowhere near the success they had in 1934.

Within a few years, the Stars began to encounter financial problems. Attendance declined, and the team stopped going to spring training in the South. The absence of a winning team and competitive games diminished the Stars' chances for profitable seasons, and with players going elsewhere and other teams proving to be better, the Stars were on a downhill slide.

Actually, so was the entire league, as players began jumping to teams in Cuba, Mexico, and the Dominican Republic. Dominican dictator Rafael Trujillo was especially active in recruiting not only black players but also white players from Major League Baseball. To make matters worse, during a trip to Cleveland in

1937, the Stars' bus rolled over, injuring a number of players, some of whom had to be hospitalized.

The Stars were never even in contention for another championship, usually finishing in the lower half of the league standings. In 1941, they dropped to a lowly 12–26 record. Meanwhile, fans, disenchanted with Bolden and the Stars, stopped coming to their games.

In an effort to rebuild attendance, Bolden stacked the roster with local players, including Gene Benson, Bill (Ready) Cash, Stanley Glenn, Duckett, Harold Gould, and others. He also held tryouts for local semipro and amateur players. But it didn't work. Crowds often numbered in the low hundreds.

"If the Stars had a more powerful team, they would be playing to bigger crowds, including many whites who are disgusted with the antics of the A's and Phillies," wrote Harris in the *Tribune*. "If a man can sit home and get almost all the thrills and joys of baseball competition, he is not too apt to jump up and run to the game," he added, referring to games now being broadcast on radio. The Stars' future, he said, "looked bleak."

By the mid-1930s and early 1940s, many new figures were attracting the attention of black sports fans everywhere: boxers Joe Louis and Bob Montgomery; track star Jesse Owens; Satchel Paige; George Gregory, the first black All-American football player; Emlen Tunnell, who would become the first black NFL player inducted into the Hall of Fame; and the Harlem Globetrotters, among others. Consequently, games that were played solely among African Americans were rapidly losing their appeal.

And when Jackie Robinson broke the color barrier in 1947 and joined the Brooklyn Dodgers, with others such as Larry

Doby, Monte Irvin, and Willie Mays entering the big leagues soon afterward, black fans in large numbers jumped over to the ballparks of Major League Baseball.

Gottlieb, mindful that the team made more money with home games than it did on the road, generally kept his team from traveling. The Stars played many games at Shibe Park, as well as at Wilmington Park, owned by Phillies president Bob Carpenter and his family, and in Chester and Camden—all ballparks close enough for local fans to attend. Many of the teams the Stars played were white semipro teams whose schedules Gottlieb arranged.

With what was always a short league schedule, Bolden and Gottlieb seldom let the team rest. "Some years, we played 200 games," said Glenn, a Stars catcher in the 1940s and later a player in the Boston Braves farm system. "We often played three times a day. We'd play a doubleheader at Parkside, then drive to Baltimore for a night game." According to Glenn, the Stars also played in eastern Pennsylvania towns where large numbers of white fans attended the games, such as Doylestown, Warminster, Norristown, Souderton, and Stroudsburg, "and every place in between."

The Stars rarely played below the Mason-Dixon Line. "Playing in the South was terrible," Duckett, a former infielder, said. "The KKK made it very tough on blacks." And, he added, players often had to sleep at night in the reclining seats of their bus because they weren't allowed into hotels, and eat in the bus because they weren't allowed into restaurants. They'd also have to change into their uniforms either in the bus or under the stands.

"One time, Gottlieb scheduled us for a 28-day road trip," recalled Cash, a catcher in the 1940s who also played in the Chicago White Sox farm system. The bus in which the team was traveling, he said, blew out its engine three times along the way. Most of the trip was in the South, and players had to bear the abuse of racists who, Cash said, "would yell, 'Nigger' or 'I'm going to shoot you.'"

With future Hall of Famer Oscar Charleston now managing the Stars and living in Chester, one particularly interesting game was played in 1946 in the Tacony section of Philadelphia at a ballfield owned by Disston Saw Mill Company, which had made guns for World War II. The opponent was a white semipro team from that area. In the game, the Tacony pitcher, a five-foot-six left-hander named Bobby Shantz, struck out 17 Stars, but lost, 3–2, on an unearned winning run.

Shantz, who six years later was named the American League's Most Valuable Player, with a 24–7 record, while playing for the Philadelphia Athletics, was paid $35 for the game. "I remember when I was warming up," he recalled some 70 years later, "that the Stars players were laughing at me because I was so small. They were funny as hell, telling jokes and laughing. I never pitched against any other black team, so this was a lot of fun. They were a very nice group of guys."

"Plus," said the 16-year Major League Baseball veteran, "they were very good players. They were right at the Major League Baseball level. I recall Biz Mackey because he really stood out as a player and was also a very nice guy. He could have played in the majors, no question about it."

The Stars played in the NNL until it folded after the 1947 season. Then they lost their lease at Penmar Park, and it was torn down in 1948. In 1949, as the Stars played in the short-lived National American League (NAL) as well as a lot of independent ball, many of their home games were on Monday nights at Shibe Park. But even in the NAL, which consisted mostly of midwestern and southern teams, the Stars were never in contention for a pennant. By then, they were also traveling in two station wagons instead of the more expensive buses.

But with Phillies and Athletics games now being televised, the many limitations of World War II having ended, and integration slowly emerging, black baseball was no longer as popular with its fans as it previously had been. Attendance at Negro League games decreased considerably.

In addition, after Albert (Happy) Chandler became commissioner of Major League Baseball in 1945, the color barrier was knocked down, and black players moved out of the Negro Leagues because they could get more money in what was known as "organized baseball."

In 1945, the Stars' Marvin Williams became one of the first black players to get a Major League Baseball tryout, when he worked out with the Boston Red Sox, who did not offer him a contract. Shortly afterward, Gottlieb and Bolden began selling their players' rights to MLB. Among the first to go were outfielder Harry (Suitcase) Simpson to the Cleveland Indians and shortstop Frank Austin to the New York Yankees. Another player who went was outfielder Benson, a prominent local player who later became the last minor-league roommate of Jackie Robinson.

Bolden, still living in Darby, died of a heart attack in 1950 at the age of 68. His will, filed at the Delaware County Courthouse, showed that his interest in the Stars was valued at $1,000, and his entire estate was worth $12,810.14. Shortly thereafter, Gottlieb purchased most of Bolden's shares in the Stars from Bolden's daughter, Dr. Hilda Bolden Slie.

With gate receipts dropping to as low as $50 per game, and despite Paige joining the Stars with a one-month contract during the 1950 season, Gottlieb and Dr. Slie folded the team after the 1952 campaign. After 20 years, one of the most noteworthy teams in Philadelphia's black baseball history had ceased to exist. It was a sad time for many loyal fans.

Many years later, during a tribute paid to the team when an exhibit was erected across the street from the Stars' old ballpark on Belmont Avenue in West Philadelphia, Phillies president David Montgomery made the perfect assertion. "The legacy of the Philadelphia Stars," he said, "is one that should be passed on from generation to generation."

Negro League players for the Royal Giants, who played in Japan in 1927,
included Neil Pullen, Bill Johnson, and Biz Mackey, shown here with manager
Lonnie Goodwin (whose name was misspelled in the original photo label).
(Biz Mackey Foundation.)

• • •

6

◆ ◆ ◆

ELEVATING BASEBALL
IN JAPAN

When the chance to play on a traveling team came along, Biz Mackey was never one to reject the opportunity. As a result, Mackey played in a variety of locations outside the United States during his career, as well as on both sides of the country.

He played in Cuba, Mexico, Venezuela, Hawaii, Korea, China, the Philippines, and, most notably, in Japan, where most reports say he went in three different trips. It was in Japan that he forever etched his name in the country's baseball history.

Mackey began his worldwide travels in 1925, playing in the Cuban Winter League with a club called Almendares. He played in Japan in 1927, 1932, and 1935. On Mackey's last Pacific trip, his team played games in Hawaii, the Philippines, and China before landing in Japan.

Each time, his presence in Japan proved to be particularly significant because of the role he played in helping to increase baseball's popularity to a much higher level than it had been. In fact, in the long history of Japanese baseball, Mackey often comes up as one of the key figures in the advancement of the sport to its present level.

A version of baseball had been played in Japan since 1872, when a U.S. teacher named Horace Wilson introduced the game to his students. Soon, teams began forming, and eventually the game was played by Japanese high school and college students using a smaller baseball, smaller fields, and a smaller strike zone than those used in the United States. But Japanese baseball didn't share the popularity of sports such as sumo wrestling, judo, and karate. Even track and field, ice skating, cricket, rugby, and rifle shooting were higher on the popularity list than baseball.

The first foreign team ever to play in Japan was an amateur team from Hawaii in 1907. Soon afterward, college teams from the United States began traveling to Japan. And in 1908 a team of professional players called the Reach All-Americans went there. This group was set up by Al Reach, one of the first professional players in baseball and later the owner of the Philadelphia Phillies and the A. J. Reach Company, a major sporting-goods manufacturer. In a series of exhibition games called "The Oriental Tour," the team performed in Hawaii and the Philippines as well as in Japan, where it won all 17 games it played against top Japanese college teams.

Those setbacks resulted in an "ego-crushing experience for Tokyo's top collegiate players," according to Sayuri Guthrie-Shimizu (2012) in her book *Transpacific Field of Dreams.* In particular, a perfect game by a Reach pitcher cemented the young Japanese team's mental demolition.

But the country's fledgling interest in baseball made a quick recovery as increasingly better players and teams emerged. Japan's affinity for the game really began to grow in 1913 with the arrival of a team of Major Leaguers on a worldwide tour from the United States. Led by New York Giants manager John Mc-Graw and including players such as Tris Speaker, Sam Crawford, and Jim Thorpe, this group toured the country, playing against Japanese amateur and college teams. Thorpe, having just won worldwide acclaim for his Olympic performance in 1912, was hugely popular with the local fans.

Along the way, other college and semipro teams traveled from the United States to Japan. Then, in 1920, the first Japanese professional teams and league were formed. The league lasted until 1923, when it disbanded due largely to a lack of interest and funds.

A team of Major League Baseball all-stars led by Waite Hoyt, Bullet Joe Bush, and Casey Stengel played in Japan in 1922 and won its first six games by a combined 58–1 score. Then controversy erupted when they allegedly threw the seventh game. That same year, a team from Yale University also played in Japan.

Three years later, a women's team known as the Philadelphia Bobbies visited the country. Playing third base was a 13-year-old Philadelphian named Edith Houghton, later to become a star in women's baseball, an officer in the U.S. Navy during World War II, and a scout for the Phillies—the first woman scout in Major League Baseball history.

The Bobbies, mostly in their teens or early 20s, played men's teams in Japan and later Korea following a cross-country tour of the United States. Despite the addition of two former Major

Leaguers to the squad, the Bobbies won only two of 11 games in Japan while generating little excitement among the local fans.

Thereafter, however, the sport increased in popularity only slowly until 1927. That's when Mackey and 13 fellow Negro Leaguers made their first trip to Japan.

It is worth noting that the reports and studies on this and future trips vary in regard to the dates of the trips and the level of influence attributed to both the Negro League and Major League Baseball teams on the elevation of baseball in Japan. Moreover, the Negro League events were given little coverage by U.S. publications and information was scarce until recent decades, when an increasing number of journalists began in-depth studies of the trips.

According to Lawrence Hogan, writing in *Shades of Glory—The Negro Leagues and the Story of African American Baseball*, "The spring trip to Japan by Raleigh 'Biz' Mackey and his friends could have been celebrated—as indeed it might well have been at the decade's beginning—as one more sign of the wonderful international reach of black professional baseball. Yet, the national weeklies characterized the trip as damaging to the league structure that was already under assault from forces that would bring it down."

Whether or not it was true that international barnstorming was bad for black baseball is another issue. In any case, an outstanding 1927 team, named the Philadelphia Royal Giants, was assembled by promoter Lonnie Goodwin, the club's manager and widely considered one of the leading skippers of his era. Starting in California, where it first played in a mostly white winter league, the new team romped through its schedule, posting a 26–11–1 record and winning the pennant. The group, considered one of the best African American teams ever put together, also included future Hall of Famers Bullet Joe Rogan, Turkey Stearnes, Bill Foster, Willie Wells, and Andy Cooper. Mackey was the team's captain.

By then, Kenso Zenimura, the manager of a team of Japanese Americans who played in the California league under the name of Fresno Athletic Club, had been asked to play some games in Japan. Zenimura, a native of Japan, invited the Royal Giants to go with them. Since baseball was becoming more popular in Japan, both managers considered it a chance to make some good money. So the trip was scheduled.

When the California season ended in late winter, the Royal Giants boarded a ship and, 19 days later, arrived in Japan. There were a few changes in the roster when Rogan, Stearnes, and Wells headed home, but Mackey, Rap Dixon, Frank Duncan, Cooper, and the others stayed with the team. When they arrived, they became the first Negro League team ever to appear in the Land of the Rising Sun. Moreover, for the first time, they made Japanese fans aware that baseball in the United States was not just a game for white people.

Landing in April 1927, the Royal Giants played their first game against Fresno in the newly built Meiji Shrine Stadium, one of the biggest ballparks in Japan. In that first game, with a then-Japanese-record crowd of 10,000 in attendance, Mackey, playing shortstop, became the first player ever to hit a ball over the new stadium's center field fence, some 427 feet from home plate. It flew "like an arrow," wrote one Japanese writer. "The fans were ecstatic and loudly applauded the blow."

"Mackey, the star shortstop of his team, was the heaviest slugger of the day, getting three safeties on four official trips to the diamond, one being a four-ply wallop, and the other two, a three sacker and a double," said another newspaper account of the game. "His homer whistled through the air and landed without a drop on the center field bleachers, and then rolled out of sight some hundred feet into a clump of trees, thus establishing a record for long-distance slamming since the opening of the ball ground. On trotting home to the plate, he met with a tremendous ovation from the crowd and he surely thanked the lucky stars for the thriller he got off Mamiya [the opposing pitcher]," extolled the *Japan Times*.

Mackey would go on to hit three balls over the fence at another ballpark known as Jingu Stadium: one in left field, one in right, and one in center. Although they were still using "dead balls" in Japan, the balls were said to travel farther than any Japanese player could expect to hit one. In fact, the next time a hitter would smash a ball over Jingu Stadium's center field fence was when Babe Ruth did it in 1934.

The Royal Giants went on to play 23 games in Japan. In one game, U.S. Consul General Steven Miller from Ithaca, New York, threw out the first ball.

While traveling throughout the country to meet teams that were largely less skilled, the Royal Giants demonstrated a brand of high-quality baseball that was noticed by more than just the fans. The Japanese players, too, tended to stand and watch in awe as their opponents warmed up on the sidelines.

"I never faced a more impressive team than that black team," said longtime Japanese player and manager Saburo Yokozawa in a 1983 interview by Japanese baseball writer Kazuo Sayama for his article "Black Gentle Giants" (1986). "None before and none after. I still remember the faces of some players—Dixon, Mackey.

It was a strange team. When we played, we only had big surprises. First, they impressed us by their power. Their moves were elastic. Speedy and strong. We were convinced that we had no chance to win."

"They were so big," said Japanese pitcher Shozo Wakahara. "We talked among us that they were twice bigger than we were. I could manage to go against other strong teams, but I couldn't against the PRG [Philadelphia Royal Giants]. We knew that we would lose even before the game [started]."

The U.S. players also put on a show after every game that was extremely popular with the fans. They played "shadow ball," staging an infield drill by whipping an imaginary ball around the infield. Outfielder Dixon of the Harrisburg Giants gave base-running exhibitions, circling the bases with lightning speed, as well as throwing demonstrations, tossing balls over the fence from home plate.

Mackey, who Guthrie-Shimizu (2012) said "immortalized his play in Japan" with his home runs, participated, too. Biz, who was said to have bragged that he could throw a ball from home plate to the bank of the seats behind the center field fence, would fire a ball from behind the plate to second base in his usual squatting position. "We were simply surprised at his hard throwing," wrote Sayama. "But once the games began, he didn't do that. After catching balls, he stood up and threw in quite a fundamental way."

Mackey also played shortstop in some of the games, an example of versatility that amazed the home fans. "In fielding, Mackey at shortstop is above the rest," said a high school coach, Suishu Tobita.

Although the Royal Giants won all but one of the 23 games they played—the one loss coming on a highly disputed call by an umpire—unlike some previous U.S. teams that had played in Japan, as well as the later Major League Baseball squad led by Ruth, they never tried to run up the score or demean the opposition. Not wanting to insult the local fans or take away their interest in a game, which in other years had created smaller and smaller crowds as the U.S. teams whipped the locals by large margins, the Giants always tried to keep the scores close, avoiding humiliating the opposing team and the fans.

After their wins, the Negro League players, who did not act cocky or showboat about their accomplishments, made an enormously favorable impression on the Japanese people and players, one of whom said that his team "was extremely pleased to find that they did not take an overbearing attitude." "The Japanese appreciated that," said one local writer. "They [the Negro Leaguers] were really gentlemen."

Everyone on the Japanese side deeply appreciated the Negro Leaguers' sportsmanship and thoughtful and kind approach to the competition, and consequently gave them the best possible treatment during their stay on the island. In the long run, the Negro League players' good manners and the respect they showed for their hosts also helped to strengthen the Japanese people's interest in the game.

Said one of the Japanese players, Yasuo Shimaza: "Some players from other teams made several kinds of funny shows. Some danced around before the spectators and made strange sounds like those made by fowls. The Royal Giants didn't display any of these deeds. One American player said, 'I like Japanese people. There is no racial barrier here. What a good country. I'd like to come back again.'"

Their gracious behavior and good manners were heavily emphasized when a bad call by an umpire took a run away from the Giants. Although they protested, the umpire refused to reverse the call. As it turned out, the Giants lost the game by one run, their only loss in Japan. Not raising a big fuss about it once again raised the classy behavior of the Giants in the eyes of the fans.

Their personal relationships off the field were particularly good, too. The Negro Leaguers freely socialized with the local people, most of whom had never seen a black person before. There was a great feeling of camaraderie, according to Sayama, who said that the Giants, especially Mackey, provided the inspiration for the start of pro baseball in Japan.

"They are calm and quiet on the field and at their hotel," wrote Yakyu Kai in a 1927 issue of *Baseball World*. "They talk to each other in small voices. We can't tell if they are there or not. If you ask about games, they are very humble."

In the trip, often known as "The 1927 Goodwill Tour," the Royal Giants were superb diplomats, helping to solidify relations between Japan and the United States as countries. Of equal significance, the Negro Leaguers, who stayed at the best hotels, faced no racial barriers as they often did at home. They were treated equally, sometimes even like royalty. That gave the Negro Leaguers a sense of freedom that they seldom experienced in the United States. Mackey and his teammates were most appreciative.

In addition, the touring players were never reluctant to give lessons or share their knowledge of how to play the game. Mackey and Duncan of the Kansas City Monarchs were especially willing to show their hosts the finer points of baseball, a practice that again led to the country's boundless acceptance of its U.S. visitors.

No one was more popular for his gentlemanly conduct than Mackey. Combining this comportment with his obvious ability, Mackey proved to be a major inspiration not only to the fans but also to the future development of baseball in Japan. In later years, Japanese baseball historians often credited Mackey as being the primary figure who helped to elevate baseball to a much higher level.

The fans loved Mackey. And so did the opposing players. He was so highly regarded, in fact, that once when he was hit by a ball thrown by Wakahara, the Japanese pitcher bowed down to him. Mackey bowed back, grinned, and ran to first base.

Mackey also formed a connection with Emperor Hirohito, then in his second year as the head of a rapidly growing country. At one point, Hirohito even presented a trophy to the visiting squad, and his enthusiasm about the Negro Leaguers also played a major role in raising Japanese interest in baseball at a professional level. Of course, Hirohito later ordered Japan's bombing of Pearl Harbor and, with his country's entry into World War II, became a militant and hated enemy of the United States.

Ultimately, the Royal Giants' trip, including brief stops in China, Korea, and Hawaii and a tour record of 35–2–1, ended after nearly two months, and in late May, the team was back in the United States. But the Eastern Colored League had instituted a ruling under which all players would be suspended for five years if they went to Japan or elsewhere and were unavailable to play with their regular teams. Because they had missed spring training and part of the regular season, Mackey and his teammates were punished accordingly and left without a place to play.

Eventually, however, when fans saw Mackey seated in the stands during a game at Hilldale Park, chief operator and manager Ed Bolden reduced the suspension to two months. Biz was back in the lineup in late July, returning to the good graces of his team and fans.

But Mackey's travels were far from over. In 1929, he was still playing with Hilldale when the Great Depression struck down the world's economy. Negro League baseball was shut down, and that season players were left to find salaries on their own. Many formed teams and barnstormed wherever they could find games.

Mackey joined a group of black players, including Hilldale teammates George (Tank) Carr and Ping Gardner, and traveled to Hawaii, where they played local teams for two months. Hilldale played again in 1930, but because the players hadn't returned by the start of the season, Bolden claimed that he would suspend his absent players for one game for each day they were absent. Mackey was out of action for a few months before he returned to the Hilldale lineup.

Biz stayed home for the next few years, but during the 1932 season he joined another Royal Giants team that played in Japan, the Philippines, and Hawaii. That team included Cooper, Carr, Halley Harding, a Cuban pitcher named Javier Perez, and an assortment of other lesser-known Negro Leaguers.

By then, the Great Depression was in high gear, and teams were getting increasingly into financial trouble. They had less and less money, not only for players' salaries but also for their travel to spring training. Accordingly, players quit their current teams and went anywhere else where they could earn a sustainable living. One such place was Japan, where the global depression had been less pronounced.

"It can't be denied that the reason Mackey came back to Japan was the Depression as well as his love of Japan," Sayama wrote. The team went on to post a 24–1–1 record, giving them a 46–2–1 record overall from their two trips to Japan. "Mackey's amiable personality showed the highest level of baseball at that time," Sayama wrote.

Again, Mackey made a favorable impression with his catching abilities. An opposing catcher, a college student named Kazuo Usami, said: "I was a catcher, and looked very carefully at his play. He was so good. He threw without standing up a second. That was my first time to see such a strong arm. My eyes were on his mitt. Our mitt didn't have net. You had to use both hands when catching a ball, otherwise the ball popped out. Mackey catched [sic] a ball smoothly with one hand. It was beauty. I was suddenly awakened to see his catching. I guess he had a big impact on catchers in Japan."

In the early winter after the 1934 season, by which time he was a member of the Philadelphia Stars and had helped the team win its first and only Negro National League championship, Mackey signed up for another trip. Although records are scarce, John Holway and the Baseball Hall of Fame indicate that this team, which included Rogan, Duncan, Chet Brewer, and Newt Allen, went back to Japan, getting paid $3,000 apiece in addition to a percentage of the gate receipts. During the trip, they also played in China, the Philippines, and Hawaii.

Although the trip stretched into 1935, the players arrived home in time to start their seasons with their teams. It would be the last time Mackey went abroad. But it was a worthwhile trip for him. In addition to the baseball part of this visit, Biz met his future wife, Lucille.

Born in Japan, Lucille was the child of an African American father and a Japanese mother. A relative of hers was responsible for housing and taking care of the Giants' needs when they were in Japan. At one point, this relative introduced Lucille to Biz. The couple became friends and, becoming increasingly fond of each other, dated frequently. Biz was said to have been "overwhelmed by her beauty."

After Biz returned home, the two frequently wrote to each other. But they lost touch when World War II began, and the romance seemed to be over. It would resurface, however, some years later.

Meanwhile, once again, the presence of the Negro Leaguers had a major influence on Japanese baseball. More and more college and professional teams were formed, and the quality of the game increased considerably.

Major League Baseball also played a large role in building enthusiasm for the sport among the Japanese fans. In addition to the 1913 tour, big-league teams traveled to Japan in 1931, 1932, and 1934. The most noteworthy of these was the 1934 squad, which included not only Lou Gehrig, Jimmie Foxx, Charlie Gehringer, and Lefty Gomez but also Babe Ruth, who was close to the end of his famous career.

Ruth had been reluctant to make the trip, which was called "Connie Mack's World Tour" because it had been arranged by the Philadelphia Athletics icon. In fact, originally, he had flat-out refused to go. Eventually, though, he went and, of course, was a huge attraction among the Japanese fans, who followed him everywhere he went and showered him with gifts as he paraded down the streets. U.S. ambassador Joseph Grew called Ruth "a more effective ambassador than I could ever be."

Also on the team, much to the bewilderment of fans and other players, was Moe Berg, a reserve catcher. Few knew why Berg had been placed on the team. But it turned out that he was an undercover agent for the forerunner of the Central Intelligence Agency and was there to photograph strategic areas of Japan. His photos were later used in World War II by General Jimmy Doolittle when he led the attack on Tokyo.

Although they were met by an estimated 100,000 fans and paraded down the street when they originally arrived in Japan, and they attracted 60,000 to their first game, Ruth and his teammates didn't conduct themselves in the mannerly way the Negro Leaguers had. The all-white big-league team "treated fans and opponents with contempt, running up scores and insulting their hosts both on and off the field," said Zenimura. "On one rainy day, Ruth, who was also the team's manager, played first base holding a parasol. Gehrig wore rubber boots. Al Simmons lay down in the outfield grass while the game was in progress."

On the other hand, many reports said that the big leaguers were widely lauded by the Japanese during their 18 games, as had happened during each previous visit, and did yeoman service in increasing the interest of the game. But some later accounts said that the team left a bad impression on its hosts with what was described as "rowdy behavior." That was not true of the Negro Leaguers, who, as recorded throughout the sport's history, played a major role in bringing top-quality baseball to Japan.

"Negro League baseball helped elevate the level of play of Japanese baseball during its three trips to Japan," said noted current sports writer Yoichi Nagata. To that, Sayama added: "If we had seen only the [M]ajor [L]eaguers, we might have been discouraged and disillusioned by our poor showing. What saved us was the tours of the Philadelphia Royal Giants, whose visits gave Japanese players confidence and hope."

In 1936, the Japanese Baseball League was formed. But relations between Japan and the United States were already deteriorating. They collapsed as World War II approached and remained this way well after the war had ended. Meanwhile, baseball became virtually nonexistent in Japan, except when it was played behind bars, in the prisons where much of the country's military had been placed during the U.S. takeover.

Following the end of the war, though, many U.S. servicemen were stationed in Japan. The group included a number of Major League Baseball players who had joined the military. With their help and with memories left by the exhibition tours of prior years, baseball eventually made a comeback.

Ultimately, with the help of the United States during the first half of the 20th century, baseball eventually reached the point where it was Japan's number one sport. The game flourished at all levels. In fact, when foreign players were first allowed to join Japanese professional teams in the 1950s, black players were among the first to be admitted.

Now, professional baseball thrives in Japan. In the 1960s, a player named Sadaharu Oh came on the scene and ultimately became a world-famous power hitter who earned the nickname "Home Run King." By the 1990s, Japanese players were joining Major League Baseball in the United States. The first Japanese player of note to perform in the big leagues was pitcher Hideo Nomo with the Los Angeles Dodgers in 1995. Numerous players have performed in the majors since then, leading up to the present. As of this writing, outfielder Icharo Suzuki has played in the United States for 17 years while becoming one of baseball's top hitters.

That might not have happened had it not been for Biz Mackey and his Negro League teammates, who went to Japan and helped to launch the game to its present heights.

Joe DiMaggio (second from left) shakes hands with Mackey (right),
one of his favorite players. Jesse Hubbard (left) and Soldier Boy Semler
are also shown here. (NoirTech Research, Inc.)

◆ ◆ ◆

7

. . .

MOVING UP TO THE JOB
OF MANAGER

It was no surprise when Biz Mackey was chosen to manage a Negro League team. After all, Mackey had spent nearly two decades as a professional player, and he knew the game inside and out.

Mackey was especially skilled as a catcher. He knew how to call a game, knew how to handle pitchers, and knew all the intricacies of baseball and the special nuances that were part of every good catcher's repertoire. The fact that he could still hit made his candidacy all the more appealing to teams who preferred player-managers.

An equally significant factor was that as a young player, Mackey had come under the tutelage of Hall of Fame player, manager, and executive Rube Foster. A native Texan himself, Foster had always gone out of his way to teach youngsters from his home state the finer points of the game, and Biz was fortunate enough to have been able to hang around Foster and learn firsthand about the game from this icon of Negro League baseball. Foster, of course, had been one of the greatest pitchers in Negro League history, with his career including a stint with the Philadelphia Giants in the early 1900s. Among his other noteworthy credits were his interest in player development and his willingness to teach young players the finer points of the game.

Biz had also worked through much of his career helping other players, especially younger ones still learning the skills of professional baseball. "He could help a ballplayer to become a better ballplayer," said Nap Gulley of the Newark Eagles, while emphasizing that Mackey was one of the finest managers for whom he had ever played. "He was a great manager," added Hall of Famer Buck O'Neil, a standout Negro League player for nearly 20 years. Mackey had taken an indirect path to his place as a Negro League manager. By the end of that journey, though, he wound up piloting teams for all or parts of nine seasons between 1936 and 1947, winning one championship.

Biz was still playing with the Philadelphia Stars in 1935, but injuries had inevitably started to lead to the deterioration of his game. At the end of the season, Stars boss Ed Bolden decided to unload those on the team who he didn't think were sufficiently productive. Mackey was one of them. During the winter of 1936, Biz was traded to the Columbus (Ohio) Elite Giants for outfielder Roy Parnell and pitcher Sad Sam Thompson.

Mackey never set foot in Columbus. The team, after playing only one year there, was moved by owner Tom Wilson to Washington, where it continued to be called the Elite Giants. Regaining his health and enthusiasm, Mackey spent the 1936 season in Washington with the Negro National League club, hitting .291 in 31 games and restoring his catching versatility. Observers said that Biz "was playing his best game of ball in some years." The

Washington Tribune said, "Mackey has been a bulwark of power on defense and offense."

During the 1936 season, Mackey got his first taste of managing when Wilson named him the team's interim skipper to fill in for Jim (Candy) Taylor while Taylor and four other Washington players left the team to participate in a tournament in Denver. Mackey managed the Elite Giants for three weeks before Taylor returned to resume his duties.

In 1937, Mackey was back in command. This time, Taylor had left the team for good, moving on to manage the Chicago Americans. Mackey was named the Elite Giants' full-time manager. All the while, Biz was still playing, and he was still considered to be the league's best all-around catcher. "He is a dangerous hitter at all times and ranks with the best in handling pitchers," sports writer Art Carter of the *Afro-American* declared. Mackey ended the season with a .241 batting average in 27 games.

That summer, fans emphasized Mackey's popularity by voting him as the manager of the East squad, beating out Oscar Charleston, in the 1937 East-West Negro League All-Star Game. With teammate Bill Wright getting three hits, Biz's team captured a 7–2 decision.

Also at the end of that season, a Negro National League all-star team led by Mackey defeated a team called the Trujillo All-Stars, which had a lineup that featured Cool Papa Bell, Josh Gibson, and Sam Bankhead. Johnny Taylor pitched a no-hitter for Mackey's team as it beat Satchel Paige and the Dragons before a crowd of 22,500 at the Polo Grounds in New York.

The following year, Wilson, a man seemingly always on the move, packed up his team and moved it to Baltimore, where it would reside for the next 13 years. The son of two physicians and a wealthy owner of businesses, farms, and nightclubs, Wilson had earlier versions of the Elite Giants stationed at both Cleveland and Nashville and, for three decades, would be one of the most powerful figures in Negro League baseball. Now one of the mainstays of the organization, Mackey went with him as the team's manager.

In 1938, judging by the skimpy statistics available today, the Elite Giants were mired in the middle of the Negro National League standings, just as they had been in previous years. Mackey, however, was still one of the stars of the league, even though he was 41 years old. While hitting .283 in 29 games, Mackey was once again the starting catcher for the East in the Negro League All-Star Game. He went 0-for-4 in a 5–4 West victory.

Mackey, still at the top of the list among Negro League catchers, took a young backstop under his wing to teach him the rudiments of the game. The youngster, a Philadelphia teenager named Roy Campanella, would take to Mackey's teachings so well that eventually he eclipsed his mentor's renown and became the second African American (after Jackie Robinson) elected to the Baseball Hall of Fame (see Chapter 8).

Meanwhile, although the Elite Giants' performance had been mostly mediocre, that ended in 1939. Biz wound up hitting .338 in 27 games, while Baltimore reached the Negro National League playoffs. After finishing third during the regular season with a 25–21 record, the Elite Giants defeated the Eagles in the opening series, then blanked the first-place Homestead Grays in two games to win the league championship.

But by that point in 1939, Mackey had taught himself out of a job. The youthful Campanella had become the club's starting catcher, and although Biz still had a lot left to give, he was 42 years old and decidedly on the down side of his career. After the season, Wilson replaced him as manager with 15-year veteran Negro League player George Scales, a hot hitter with an equally hot head, and sold Biz's rights to the Newark Eagles.

The *Newark Herald* was ecstatic. "He has long been known to be the best developer of young hurlers, and with only one veteran pitcher, Leon Day, on the staff, the services of Mackey are badly needed," the newspaper crowed.

The Eagles were on the verge of becoming one of the most prominent Negro League teams. Owned and operated by Abe and Effa Manley, the team had been moved from Brooklyn to Newark in 1936.

Effa, a Philadelphia-born half-black half-Caucasian woman and later a civil rights activist, lived first in West Philadelphia and then in the South section of the city. She graduated from Penn Central High School and was an avid follower of the Hilldale Daisies, making friends with some of the players, including Mackey. After high school, Effa—who was known as "young, smart, and beautiful"—had moved to Harlem, where she fought for integration and often traveled to Yankee Stadium to watch her favorite player (Babe Ruth) and team (the Yankees).

Ultimately, she met Abe, 24 years her elder, who had lived in recent years in Camden, New Jersey. Abe Manley had become owner of a minor-league team called the Camden Leafs, and he, too, had memories of following the Hilldale team and becoming friends with Mackey. After marrying Abe, who had sold the Leafs and formed the Newark team by consolidating the Brooklyn Eagles and the Newark Dodgers, Effa became deeply involved in the operation of the Eagles. She handled most of the

The Newark Eagles were regarded as one of the more prominent Negro League teams when Mackey (front row, third from right) was their manager.
(Biz Mackey Foundation.)

club's activities, including business affairs and personal and public relations. She did it so successfully that in 2006, she became the first woman elected to the Baseball Hall of Fame.

Effa, who always attended league meetings and often made her feelings known through fiery dialogue, was originally one of Mackey's biggest fans. "When it was late in the game, and the pitcher had stopped all our good hitters and just one hit was needed, I'd say, 'Mackey, go in there and hit that ball,'" she once said.

Despite his advancing age, Biz did just that, hitting .309 in 37 games during the 1940 season. But in 1941, the always-dominating Effa made an addition to his resume by naming him manager of the Eagles, replacing Dick Lundy. Mackey continued to play, too, of course, often putting himself in the lineup at first base as well as behind the plate.

Mackey was well liked by virtually all of his players. A nonsmoker who at the time had become a nondrinker, he was also a special role model, particularly for the young players on his teams.

"You couldn't find a better guy to be around," second baseman Sammy Hughes told John Holway (1988) for his book *Blackball Stars*. "He'd give you everything he had at all times. On the field and off. He was a prince of a man."

To this, Frank (Doc) Sykes, a longtime pitcher who played against Mackey during six seasons and later worked for many years as a dentist in Baltimore, added, "He was a wonderful general in running the team."

Over the next two years, Mackey, fueled by his brilliant knowledge of the game and his superb abilities as a leader, guided the Eagles to second-place (19–11) and fourth-place (19–17) finishes in the Negro National League.

One of his star players was a young shortstop by the name of Monte Irvin, who had been with the team since 1937. "When he was chosen as manager of the Newark Eagles, we were all very happy," Irvin recalled. "We knew his reputation. He was the dean of teachers. We also knew how great he'd been as a catcher. I played shortstop, but Biz eventually moved me to center field. That was a pretty smart move. I spent the rest of my career in the outfield."

"He was a good manager," added Irvin, who went on to become one of the first African American players in Major League Baseball and eventually a member of the Hall of Fame and an executive in the baseball commissioner's office. "He could evaluate players better than anybody I've ever seen. Amazingly, sometimes he'd catch, too. 'I can hit this pitcher, so I'll catch today,' he'd say. Or he'd say, 'I need to catch this pitcher of ours, so I'll be the catcher today.'"

Irvin told a story about sidearm pitcher Max Manning: "One day before a game, Biz said, 'Max, we're going to throw very few curves today. I know what I'm doing.' Max threw three curveballs in the entire game and won, 5–0. Biz knew what to call and where to call for it. He knew what moves to make. We had only 16 or 17 players on the team in those days. A guy might pitch one game, then play right field or first base in the next game. As a manager, you had to know how to switch your players around and how to make out your lineups. Biz was a master at doing that."

Biz was also a master at staying calm. A jovial person most of the time, he rarely argued or got thrown out of games. Once in 1940, however, he got into a dispute with umpire Fred Mc-Crary. Biz hurled some uncomplimentary names at the umpire and was ejected. He was fined $10 for conduct unbecoming of a ballplayer.

In 1941, Mackey was 44 years old and wearing a size 50 uniform jersey, but still performing his duties as a player-manager. It wasn't easy for him. "I don't see how he could throw a ball," said Day. "His fingers were all broken on his right hand, which was all messed up. Still, he was a good catcher who could have caught in any league. I liked him to catch when I was pitching."

Added Campanella, "To look at his hands, you'd say, 'This guy must have been a butcher, the way his fingers were curved and broken.'" Ironically, Mackey, beloved by fans, beat Campanella by nearly 30,000 votes (209,000 to 180,000) to be elected to the East-West All-Star Game that year.

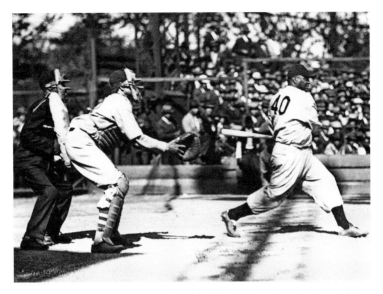

Although he had gained considerable weight, Mackey continued to play during his years as manager. (John W. Mosley Photograph Collection, Charles L. Blockson Afro-American Collection, Temple University Libraries, Philadelphia, PA.)

That winter, Mackey's career took a major turn. He got into a dispute with Effa Manley in what was apparently an unfortunate misunderstanding on the parts of both parties over the amount Mackey was supposed to be paid. She had offered him a salary of $250 per month, but Mackey refused to accept it. As a result, Effa, who by this time often quibbled with Mackey and tried to interfere with his managerial duties, dismissed Biz and named former Eagles infielder Willie Wells to replace him. Coincidentally, as a teenager, Wells used to carry Mackey's glove into the ballpark when Biz played in San Antonio.

Effa sent Mackey a letter informing him of the change. She claimed that she had "always missed [Wells]" since he left the club and that she wanted him back. "I also wanted him to man-

Player's Contract

National Negro Association of Professional Baseball Clubs

LEAGUE .... NEGRO NATIONAL

THIS AGREEMENT MADE THIS ....5th.........DAY OF ..March............... 1942...

BY AND BETWEEN .... The Newark Eagles Baseball Club ....

HEREINAFTER CALLED THE "CLUB" AND ....Raleigh Mackey................................

.....1127 East 27 St.............. OF ......Los. Angeles Calif.........................
HEREINAFTER CALLED THE "PLAYER"

1. The Club hereby agrees to pay the player for his skilled services as a baseball player during the season of 1942. which shall extend from ....May .3............... to ..Sept...3................... 1942.; a salary of $.200.00... per month, payable semi-monthly on the ...1st...... and ..15th..... days of each month during the period while this contract continues in effect between the parties hereto.

2. The Player, during the season of 1942..shall faithfully serve the Club, and must keep himself in first class physical condition and at all times conform his personal conduct and deportment, both on and off the playing field, to standards of good citizenship and good sportsmanship.

3. The Club will provide and furnish the player with transportation, board, and lodgings while "abroad", or traveling with the Club on the road or in other cities.

4. In order to fit himself for his duties under this contract, the Player agrees, at his own expense and without expense to the Club, to report for service, at least..................days before the opening of the season of the National Negro Association of Professional Baseball Clubs, which season shall be the same.as the term of this contract, the player however, to receive board and lodgings, from the Club during said training period.

5. The player shall report at the field of play, whether at home or "abroad", in uniform at least one hour before the time stated for such game to be played, and for his failure to do so he shall, at the discretion of the Club, be fined $5.00 for each infraction. The Player also agrees that he may be subjected to a fine of $10.00 for being put out of any League game by an umpire during the League season. Should a player strike an umpire before or after during a League game, he shall be fined $25.00 and suspended for the next three successive League games. If Club refuses to pay, umpire shall forfeit the game to the other Club but continue the game as an exhibition game. The fine shall then be collected and mailed, registered letter, to the Treasurer. The second offense of any player striking an umpire shall, in addition to the $25.00 fine, prohibit the player in any League game until ruled upon by the Advisory Board of League Owners.

6. In the event of failure of the Player to report for practice or to participate in any exhibition games, when requested, a penalty, by way of a fine, may be imposed by the Club, not to exceed $15.00, the same to be deducted from the compensation stipulated herein.

7. This contract may be terminated by the Club, or by any assignee of this contract by giving the player five (5) days written notice of such termination.

8. The player agrees that in the event he should be transferred to some other Club, and his contract assigned to such Club, the Club......................shall be released from any and all liability under this contract and the Player shall look to the transferee and assignee for compliance with its terms.

In case of injuries or sickness not contracted while performing duties for the Club the Player shall not be paid by the Club.

With the exception of above articles, the rules of Major Minor League shall be in effect; especially the clause which refers to betting on baseball games.

In Witness Whereof .... has annexed its common or corporate seal, duly attested by its proper officer, and the player hereunto set his hand and seal.

WITNESSES .... *Raleigh Mackey*

ATTEST ....
Effa Manley, SECRETARY

This contract subject to United States Government ruling on baseball ....

Mackey's contract with the Newark Eagles became the subject of a controversy in 1942. (NoirTech Research, Inc.)

age the team," she added. "I do not know whether or not this will surprise you, but when you left Newark last year without seeing me, I was of the opinion that you were not anxious to manage. A manager should have been interested in discussing plans for the next season at the close of last."

"Wells and I both want you to stay," she added. "I would like you to take charge of driving the bus." She promised to provide additional pay for the extra duty.

As much as he would have liked to return to Newark, Mackey declined the offer, insisting that his legs hurt, and that he was going to stay in Los Angeles, where he now lived and where he had married Lucille. He took a job with North America Aviation, a company dealing in defense work as World War II was escalating. "You should see Lucille," Mackey jokingly wrote to Effa. "She is too fat for words," which, of course, wasn't true.

Incredibly, the company asked Effa Manley to write a recommendation to help Mackey get the well-paying job. First, though, she sent a letter to Mackey, advising him of the company's request and telling him she would write the letter if Biz returned the money she had sent him for travel expenses so he could come east for the upcoming season. Mackey replied: "I would have returned had you sent me the other money I asked for. I couldn't walk back there, so I had to do the next best thing—get a job." He promised to return the money. "I have played ball twenty-two years and I haven't taken a nickel from no one, but they have taken plenty away from me. Don't worry[;] you will get your money back."

Whether or not he ever did reimburse his former boss has never been revealed. But Biz got the job with North America Aviation and stayed in Los Angeles, working his daytime job and playing at night in the California Winter League. He did that for the next three years, playing his first season with the Sea Lions of San Francisco, where a local newspaper touted him as "the Wonder Boy whose exhibition of batting, catching, throwing, and daredevil sliding has amazed fans the country over." The Sea Lions, a traveling team, performed in cities such as Helena, Montana; Charleston, West Virginia; Eau Claire, Wisconsin; and Lethbridge, Alberta.

In 1945, as the war was nearly over and the work of defense plants was coming to an end, Mackey returned to the Eagles. The often contentious Effa Manley had become involved in another dispute, this time with Wells, and she had fired him. She replaced him with Biz, paying him a salary of $400 per month, picking up his transportation costs from Los Angeles, and giving him an extra stipend of $20 per week for spring training. It was a stunning turn of events, but nonetheless one that greatly benefited Mackey.

Biz was still playing occasionally. "He couldn't run a lick," first baseman Lenny Pearson said to Holway. "He'd get a single and sort of wobble to first base. But he was an inspiration to us guys because he was old enough to be our father, and he made all of us get up and hustle a little bit more."

"He never had a bed check," third baseman Clarence (Half Pint) Israel told Holway. "But if you had a bad day, Mackey would write a note on pay day with the reason you were being docked." Once, Israel recalled, Mackey tried to make him change his batting stance. "We got into some words about it," he said. "I ran my mouth a lot. Mackey was the type who got along with everybody, so I felt kind of bad about it."

Back in Biz's corner, Effa Manley said: "The team looks very good. And Mackey is a story all by himself. It is really remarkable the ball he is playing, and the response he is getting from the team."

Among Mackey's players were not only Irvin, who had returned after a stint in military service, but also two up-and-coming young players who would later play in Major League Baseball, Larry Doby and Don Newcombe. Doby was a 22-year-old second baseman who had played with Newark in 1942–1943, then served in the Navy. While stationed in the South Pacific, he attracted the attention of the manager of the local military baseball team, and they became good friends. That manager's name was Mickey Vernon, a native of Marcus Hook, Pennsylvania, who would spend 23 years in the big leagues and become a two-time American League batting champion with the Washington Senators. Newcombe was a hard-throwing 19-year-old pitcher just out of high school. All who saw him throw quickly observed that he had great talent and a great future as a hurler.

"He [Mackey] was one of the most knowledgeable baseball men I ever knew," Newcombe related to Peter Golenbock for his book *Bums* (1984). Noting that he and Mackey had roomed together, Newcombe added, "We got along famously. He tried to counsel me like a father about taking care of myself and not cursing so much. He always used to be on me, on the bus, in the clubhouse, on the field, and in the hotels. 'Newcombe, you gotta stop cursing so much,' he would say."

Both Newcombe, who would win 14 games for the Eagles in 1945, and Doby said many times in later years that Mackey played an enormous role in their making it to the big leagues and becoming star players. Doby, the first African American to play in the American League, was eventually inducted into the Hall of Fame. It had been Mackey, along with Vernon, who first got the idea of converting Doby from second base to the outfield and later convinced Cleveland Indians general manager Hank Greenberg that he should do it.

Mackey, who often played first base, guided the Eagles to a fourth-place finish in 1945: the team had a season record of 21–17 and then lost to the Homestead Grays in postseason play. Afterward, he was named by Effa Manley to manage a team of Negro League all-stars against a squad of Major Leaguers in a five-game series, with four games played at Ebbets Field in Brooklyn and one in Newark.

Mackey put together a team that included Campanella, Irvin, Newcombe, and Wells at shortstop. The all-white Major Leaguers were managed by future Brooklyn Dodgers pilot Chuck Dressen and included a stellar team that was manned by players such as the Dodgers' Eddie Stanky, Ralph Branca, and Hal Gregg; Tommy Holmes, the 1945 batting and home runs champion from the Boston Braves; the Detroit Tigers' Virgil Trucks; the St. Louis Cardinals' Whitey Kurowski; Buddy Kerr of the New York Giants; and Frank McCormick of the Cincinnati Reds. Mackey's team, consisting of eight Newark players, lost four games by scores of 5–4, 2–1, 10–0, and 4–1 and tied the final game, which was called after five innings with a 0–0 score.

Effa Manley was furious. In his book *The Most Famous Woman in Baseball*, author Bob Luke (2011) quotes her as saying: "One thing the series showed me was how dumb our ballplayers are. The white boys looked so smart, and our men constantly showed how dumb they were. They just did not know what to do half of the time."

Manley's frustration reflected her continuing desire to see black baseball be taken seriously in comparison with the top white leagues. Toward this mission, the series did have one positive point for the Negro Leagues. After watching the game, Brooklyn general manager Branch Rickey saw enough of Campanella and Newcombe to offer them contracts with the Dodgers. Effa was displeased because there was no attempt by the Dodgers to purchase the contracts of other players from Negro League teams. But Campanella and Newcombe signed anyway, and by the next season, one year after the signing of Jackie Robinson, they were playing in the Dodgers' farm system. Soon, Newcombe would become the first outstanding black pitcher in Major League Baseball, winning Rookie of the Year honors in 1949 and becoming the National League's Cy Young Award winner and Most Valuable Player in 1956, the first time in big-league history a hurler had won both awards in the same season.

Mackey was still playing and even catching once in a while, although he was having considerable difficulty with his legs. After another battle with Manley that eventually led to his signing a two-year contract for $350 per month, Mackey reached the summit of his managerial career in 1946.

Despite an opening-day no-hitter by the Eagles' Leon Day against the Philadelphia Stars, the team had to overcome an early-season slump before coming back strongly. They slammed the highly rated New York Cubans 7–1 and 6–2 in a doubleheader before 12,000 at the Polo Grounds. The Eagles went on to win eight straight games, including a 16–2 bashing of the Homestead

Grays behind a four-hitter by Day. Later, they won three of a four-game series with the Grays, with the two teams scoring a total of 77 runs. Then they beat the Philadelphia Stars 3–0 and 5–0 in a doubleheader, which clinched the first-half title with a 25–9 record.

In the second half, the Eagles opened by dropping a two-game series to the Stars. Then, on the way back to Newark, the 10-year-old team bus broke down and had to be replaced by a chartered bus and then by players' own cars. Later, in one game, Mackey pulled the team off the field after protesting an umpire's call. Still, including a 17–3 smashing of the Grays at Wilmington, Delaware, and another doubleheader victory over the New York Cubans before 12,000 at the Polo Grounds, the Giants went on to capture the second-half title with a 22–7 record. Irvin, playing shortstop, won the league batting title with a .404 batting average, while second baseman Doby, first baseman Lennie Pearson, reserve catcher Pat Patterson, and outfielder Johnny Davis also ended up hitting .330 or above for the season.

Now, having watched the team turn in a winning direction, Effa praised her manager effusively. "Mackey is a story by himself," Effa wrote to Art Carter. "It is really remarkable the ball he is playing, and the response he is getting from the team."

After finishing with a 47–16 overall record during the season, the Eagles moved on to the Negro League World Series to face the Kansas City Monarchs, led by Satchel Paige, Buck O'Neil, and future Major Leaguers Hank Thompson, Connie Johnson, and Willard Brown. The Monarchs were generally considered the top team in Negro League baseball. In fact, Mackey told sports writers that Paige threw so hard that his fastball "could pound steak into hamburger."

With heavyweight boxing champion Joe Louis throwing out the first pitch, Kansas City won the first game at the Polo Grounds, 2–1, behind the pitching and hitting of Paige. A six-run seventh inning featuring Doby's two-run homer at the Eagles' Ruppert Stadium gave Newark a 7–4 win in Game Two. A 21-hit, 15–5 victory put the Monarchs back in the lead as the series moved to Kansas City for two games. A four-hitter by Rufus Lewis and a mammoth home run by Irvin off of Paige gave the Eagles an 8–1 victory in the fourth game.

Moving next to Chicago's Comiskey Park, Hilton Smith pitched the Monarchs to a 5–1 triumph. Back at Ruppert Stadium, Irvin's two home runs led Newark to a 9–7 win in Game Six. Then, in the deciding game, Davis's two-run single gave the Eagles a 3–2 victory and the championship.

Each player received a .45-carat diamond ring. Afterward, the team went on a barnstorming tour of the South with a sign "Negro League World Champs, 1946" hanging on the side of their bus. Along the way, they encountered a considerable amount of racist treatment by the Jim Crow bigots.

For Mackey, the championship proved to be a sparkling climax to his strenuous managerial career. Biz, who was being paid $2,250 for the season, had one final term as manager in 1947. That year, he not only managed the East team in an 8–2 All-Star Game loss but also made an appearance as a hitter, the sixth time he'd played in an All-Star tilt. Pinch-hitting for pitcher Henry Miller, he drew an intentional walk in the eighth inning, then was replaced by pinch-runner Vic Harris. "The paunchy 50-year-old manager of the East got into the fray," chortled Wendell Smith of the *Pittsburgh Courier*.

With Mackey making his final batting appearance during a

game on August 24, the Eagles won the first-half title in the Negro National League in 1947 but, after losing Doby to Cleveland in midseason, bowed to the second-half winner, the New York Cubans, in the championship round. In a controversial move, Effa Manley released Biz after the season, saying she did it "to make the team a real pennant contender."

The move came as a complete surprise to many. "He was a real good manager," said Mahlon Duckett, star second baseman for the Philadelphia Stars and Homestead Grays from 1940 to 1950. "Most of the years I was there [in the Negro Leagues], I played against him. He was just about as good as anybody."

Mackey returned permanently to California, where he continued to play ball. Meanwhile, the Negro National League folded in 1948, and the Manleys sold the Eagles to a group that moved the team to Houston. By then, with African American players increasingly moving to the previously white Major League Baseball, black baseball was in a serious decline. By the 1970s, 27 percent of all Major League Baseball players were men of color. Negro League baseball officially ended in 1952, closing what for one-half of a century had been a vital part of the U.S. sports world.

A star player with the Brooklyn Dodgers, Roy Campanella (right)
chats with Biz Mackey (left), the man who taught him the art of catching,
while Jess Hubbard (center) listens to the conversation.
(Negro Leagues Baseball Museum.)

• • •

8
· · ·

TEACHING CAMPY THE TRICKS
OF THE TRADE

stablished professional athletes are not usually known to
be teachers of younger players. That's what coaches are for.
Athletes are generally more concerned with themselves.

Biz Mackey was an exception. Of all his many assets, one
of his strongest was his ability to teach. Especially throughout
the later parts of his career as a player and then as a manager,
Mackey was always willing to take a youngster under his wing
and instruct him in the finer points of the game, and his teachings produced extremely positive results. Mackey became highly
acclaimed for his abilities as a teacher.

"He was not only good at it, but he was always happy to teach
young players the game," said Monte Irvin. "You could see, he
really enjoyed doing it."

Irvin should know. He was one of Mackey's pupils when Biz
was the player-manager and Monte was a young player with the
Newark Eagles. "I learned an awful lot from him," Irvin said.
"He played a very important role in my career."

As young players with Newark, Larry Doby and Don New-combe also took lessons from Mackey that eventually helped them to have successful big-league careers, with Irvin and Doby eventually becoming Hall of Famers. Many others, although they didn't make it into Major League Baseball, profited from Mack-ey's baseball intellect, too.

No one, however, was a bigger beneficiary of Mackey's work as a teacher than Roy Campanella. Like Mackey, Campanella was a catcher. But when he joined the Baltimore Elite Giants in 1937, Roy was just a 15-year-old youngster, with little experience and even less formal training in the art of catching. Mackey be-came his mentor and taught him how to catch. Little could any-one have imagined at the time that someday Campanella would be ranked with Bill Dickey, Mickey Cochrane, Yogi Berra, and Johnny Bench as the greatest Major League Baseball catchers of all time.

In later years, it was often said by observers of the game that watching Campanella play was like watching Mackey. "He helped me to learn everything," Campanella confirmed. "I tried to be the image of Biz Mackey. He was the master of defense of all catchers."

"Campanella had all of Mackey's moves," Hall of Famer Judy Johnson told John Holway (1988) in *Blackball Stars.* "If you saw him up there and didn't see his face, you'd swear it was Mackey. If you saw Campanella in one game and Mackey in the other, you would say Campanella caught in both games because he had all of Mackey's moves."

"Campanella even looked like Mackey," hard-hitting outfield-er-infielder Ted Page, who spent part of his 14-year career play-ing with Biz and the Philadelphia Stars, told Holway. "He was

. . . round, fat, and chubby—just like Mackey. He was Mackey made over. He had moves and everything back there. You had to notice him."

Campanella grew up in Philadelphia, where as a youngster he played stickball and other street games. By the age of nine, Roy had jobs delivering newspapers and milk, cutting grass, and helping to load his father's produce truck at 5:00 A.M. each day.

It was obvious at an early age that the young boy was smitten with the game of baseball. At the age of seven, Campy moved with his family from the Germantown section of Philadelphia to 1538 Kerbaugh Street in Nicetown. There, his bedroom was decorated with pictures of baseball players, most notably the greatest catchers of the era: Mickey Cochrane, Bill Dickey, Josh Gibson, and Biz Mackey.

An avid follower of the Philadelphia Phillies and Athletics, the young boy often attended their games, which were played at ballparks—Baker Bowl and Shibe Park—not far from where he lived. Campy even attempted several times to land a tryout with the Phillies. Once, he approached Phillies manager Hans Lobert, who then contacted the club's principal owner, Gerry Nugent, but was told the club was not interested. Reportedly, he also showed up at the ballpark one time and asked for a tryout but was rejected. Although light-skinned, Campy was turned down because of his color (his father was white; his mother was African American). The Phillies and all the other Major League Baseball teams were still practicing segregation at that time. He also traveled across town to Philadelphia Stars games, where he paid particular attention to Mackey, the team's catcher.

Roy's parents, John and Ida, weren't big supporters of Roy's interest in baseball and tried to convince him that attending school and studying hard were more important. But Campanella and his friends played baseball whenever and wherever they could, mostly walking the few blocks to Hunting Park, where pickup games were almost always taking place. Eventually, Campanella grew old enough to play with integrated local kids' teams, first with boys' club and junior high school teams and then at Simon Gratz High School and with standout boys' sandlot teams, one of which was called the Nicetown Giants. He was a catcher who showed considerable talent but one who lacked the qualities of a polished backstop.

In 1937, at the age of 15, Roy was invited to play with the Atlantic City Bacharach Giants, then a prominent African American traveling semipro team. Dropping out of high school, Campanella quickly accepted the invitation and was told he would earn $15 per game. He then spent the next few months with the team, often catching in the place of its regular backstop, manager Tom Dixon.

Campanella was now making money to play, and as such, he enjoyed the luxury of traveling with the Giants to away games and seeing up close how more experienced catchers handled themselves behind the plate.

One day that season, Bacharach and the Baltimore Elite Giants, one of the top teams in the Negro National League, were both staying at the Woodside Hotel in Harlem. Mackey, then the catcher and manager of the Baltimore team, approached Dixon in the lobby. As Campanella (1959) told the story many years later in his book *It's Good to Be Alive*, Mackey was then nearly 40 years old and was injured frequently. His playing career as a regular was winding down, and he often used backup catcher

Nish Williams in his place. But he really needed another top-level catcher, so he asked Dixon if he knew of anyone who could be a backup.

"You're standing right next to him," Dixon replied. "Biz Mackey, meet Roy Campanella." "In some ways," Roy related many years later, "it was the most important introduction of my life."

Mackey looked at Campanella, grinned as he so often did, and said to the youngster, "I've heard reports on you, Campy. You're kind of big for your size, ain't you?" To which Roy replied, "A little, maybe, but I'm a quick learner."

Soon afterward, Mackey and his team visited Philadelphia to play the Stars. Mackey asked Roy to meet him at the Attucks Hotel. Before the meeting was over, the kid catcher, who was still several months shy of his 16th birthday and had just completed his freshman year at Gratz, became a member of the Elite Giants. His journey began that night when he appeared in a doubleheader against the Stars and later boarded the Giants' bus for the next stop, launching what would eventually become a Hall of Fame career.

"Aim for the bright lights and that big money," Dixon told the youngster. "Success ain't gonna chase you. You got to go after it."

After joining the squad in July, Campanella caught some games against semipro teams, earning $60 per month. Mackey eventually used him on occasion in league games, but Roy quickly demonstrated his lack of experience and his inability to play at a professional level. Not only did the kid have trouble hitting; he experienced problems with his catching, missing balls, unable to throw out base runners—often throwing wildly—and not doing a very good job of calling pitches. Given the stiff competition in

Negro League baseball, Campy was also constantly mistreated, teased, and harassed by other members of the team, which sometimes left the innocent youngster in tears.

Yet it was clear to Mackey that Campy had all the tools to be a standout catcher. Biz could see that he was strong, he was smart, he had superb athletic ability, and he had exactly the raw talent that would make him an outstanding catcher. He just needed to learn the position at an elevated level. Mackey was convinced that Roy possessed the ability to become a star, even though he knew little about the position. It was time for Biz to start his lessons.

"Son, just watch me while you're on the bench," Roy remembered Mackey saying. "'I'll tell you what you have to do.' And that's just what he did," Campanella said. "He helped me to learn everything. He was the master."

Mackey, whose skills as a manager and leader were highly respected around the league, worked with Roy on all phases of the game. Hitting no matter what pitches were being thrown, catching balls in the dirt, snaring pop-ups, throwing out runners, using the correct footwork, taking the lead in running a game, calling the right pitches. It was not just a matter of learning the mechanical phases of the game, but the mental game, especially handling pitchers, was very much a part of Mackey's lessons, too. Mackey left nothing out.

"He would say," Campanella remembered, "'How do you think you'll ever make a catcher?' I was his boy. But he rode me unmercifully. He hammered into my head. And he didn't let up. He was the sternest, hard-ridingest coach I ever knew."

"Biz wasn't satisfied for me to do just one or two things good," Campanella added. "He wanted me to do everything good. And the only way I was going to improve myself was by working at the game . . . working . . . working . . . working. Not just playing at catching, but working the position. There were times when Biz made me cry with his constant dogging. But nobody ever had a better teacher."

According to Neil Lanctot (2011) in his book *Campy: The Two Lives of Roy Campanella*, "Mackey hammered home just how much a good defensive catcher meant to his ball club and pitching staff." Once, when pitcher Bill Boyd complained about Campanella's shortcomings, warning Mackey, "You're going to get that kid hurt back there," the crafty Biz replied, "Well, he ain't going to learn if he don't catch."

And so Roy, originally just a quiet, easily impressed youth, learned on the job. With Mackey emphasizing the defensive skills of a catcher as his top priority, Campy learned how to frame pitches, how to give a target, how to catch with his right hand in a fist, how to hold base runners, how to throw them out, and so many other essential elements of the position. It was not an easy job teaching this mere boy how to be a professional catcher.

"Mackey really took me in hand," Campanella (1959) wrote in his book. "There wasn't a time when we were together that he wasn't explaining something about catching. 'There's so much to learn about catching,' he would say. 'A good catcher is worth his weight in gold to a pitcher as well as the team. You gotta learn to handle pitchers like they were babies sometimes. Each one is different. You gotta scold some, you gotta flatter some, and you gotta mother them all. If you can do those things, son, you'll be the biggest man in the league.'"

"I took that advice to heart," Campy added. "I began to take charge, and as the season wore on, I found myself working as many games as Mackey. I improved steadily. I broadened out, became stronger, and my hitting was sharper."

"Biz gave me everything he could," he said. "He was the master. I was becoming a good instinctive catcher, doing the right thing without thinking about it. But my hitting was something else. Biz tried to get me to cut down on my swing and meet the ball better. 'Don't kill the ball,' he would say. 'Just meet it. It'll go plenty far.'"

"It took a long while before Roy mastered Mackey's tips and tricks," Lanctot (2011) wrote. But Biz "realized the boy was only going to get better with age and experience. 'In two years,' Mackey told a sports writer, 'this kid will be the best catcher in the NNL.'"

Campanella spent the rest of the 1937 season with the Elite Giants, then returned home and re-entered school. He wasn't there long. Roy dropped out of school in November, and when the next season rolled around, he became a full-time member of the Elite Giants. It was back to the learning curve with Mackey.

The lessons continued all season. The skill Mackey focused on most closely in this period was Roy's throwing. Base runners often took chances on Campy's arm, and frequently he threw wildly to a base trying to nail one of them. Slowly but surely, the kid's ability as a catcher improved. So did his hitting.

"Mackey was the dean of teachers," Irvin said. "He taught Campanella how to think like a catcher, how to set a hitter up—he'd throw his favorite pitch at a time when the hitter was not expecting it."

Mackey went to extremes to protect Campy from the veteran players who tried to intimidate the youngster, keeping the kid close all the time and scolding players who chastised him. But he was not the kind of teacher who demanded that the pupil emulate his style. Instead, he took the player's own skills and built on them. And yet "if you ever watched Campanella catch, you'd see Mackey in him," said Stanley Glenn, an able catcher himself who had played from 1944 to 1950 with the Stars and for three years after that in the Boston/Milwaukee Braves farm system.

Although he initially served as Mackey's backup, never playing in more than 20 games during each of his first three seasons, Campanella became his team's regular catcher late in the 1939 season. This time, though, he was on his own. During the season, Mackey was dismissed by Giants owner Tom Wilson, who thought Campy was now a fixture behind the plate. As it turned out, Mackey's effectiveness in teaching Campanella the tricks of the trade had cost him a job. After leaving the Elite Giants, Mackey moved to the Newark Eagles, where he became that team's manager while still demonstrating his skills as a catcher.

"I wasn't exactly left on my own, but I was left without a catcher that I admired," Campanella said in Holway's (1988) *Blackball Stars*. "Those three years with Mackey played an important role in my catching."

In 1939, Campy, hitting .214 in league games and .333 in nonleague outings, helped the Giants defeat the Homestead Grays in a four-game postseason playoff to win the NNL championship. Roy smacked five hits, including a home run, and drove in seven runs in the series.

By 1941, Campanella, who once caught three games in one day, had become the best catcher in the league, even surpassing the great Josh Gibson. That year, Campy, although only 19 years old, played in 54 games all together and hit .345 in 32 league games. He was named the Most Valuable Player in Negro League baseball's East-West All-Star Game.

Ironically, in 1941, Campanella was beaten by Mackey, who was then 44 years old, in the fan voting for the East-West All-Star Game. But from then until he played his last season for the Elite Giants in 1945—while also playing during winters in Puerto Rico, Mexico, Venezuela, or Cuba—Roy was the premier catcher in all of Negro League baseball, both as a hitter and on defense.

In league play, he hit .345, .304, .405, and .363 between 1941 and 1945. (He played all season in the Mexican League in 1943.) Overall, Campanella carried a .336 batting average in 257 Negro League games and .272 in 91 nonleague games during his eight years with the Giants.

Late in 1945, as the color barrier that had prohibited African American players from participating in Major League Baseball was being shattered, Campanella was signed to a Brooklyn Dodgers contract by Branch Rickey, the team's legendary general manager. By then, Rickey had already signed Jackie Robinson and several other black players to Dodgers contracts, making them the first team in Major League Baseball to integrate.

Roy spent the next two seasons in the minor leagues: first at Nashua, New Hampshire, where he was voted the New England League's Most Valuable Player, and then at Montreal, of the International League. Many baseball experts thought that Campanella should have been in the big leagues right away, but Rickey held him back. "Of course, he was a better catcher than that," Dodgers manager Walter Alston said later. "But he knew why he was there. He was part of Rickey's plan to integrate baseball."

Even then, Campanella was considered an important team

leader. At Nashua, whenever Alston was thrown out of a game, he appointed Roy to take his place. Later, whenever Campy held a conference on the mound with the pitcher, shortstop Pee Wee Reese would always join the group because he wanted to hear what the catcher had to say.

In 1948, after spending spring training with the Dodgers and then a stint at St. Paul, Minnesota, where he was the first African American player ever to perform in the American Association, Roy was summoned back to Brooklyn on July 9. Joining the Dodgers just a little more than one year after Jackie Robinson had become the first black player to appear in Major League Baseball in the 20th century, Campanella became the league's first black catcher and just the third African American player to enter the National League and sixth overall in the Major League.

Campanella reported to the team and was immediately inserted into the lineup in a series with the New York Giants. All Campy did in his first three games was collect nine hits, including two home runs, in 12 at-bats. At the time, the Dodgers were in last place. By Labor Day, they were in first, although they ultimately lost the National League pennant to the Boston Braves.

After joining the Dodgers, Campanella went on to a legendary big-league career, earning the Most Valuable Player award three times—in 1951, 1953, and 1955. He was selected for eight All-Star teams and led Brooklyn to five National League pennants and a World Series victory in 1955.

"He was the epitome of greatness," Newcombe, who had joined the Dodgers in 1949, told Mark Kram of the *Philadelphia Daily News.* "He was very astute. He sure as hell was smarter and a better catcher than anyone I ever knew."

Roy Campanella went on to become a three-time Most Valuable Player and one of baseball's greatest catchers. (Rich Westcott.)

One of the leaders of a Dodgers team that included three other future Hall of Famers—Robinson, Reese, and Duke Snider—as well as star players such as Gil Hodges, Carl Furillo, Carl Erskine, and Preacher Roe, Campy hit as high as .325 (in 1951) and led the league in 1953 with 142 RBI while carrying a .312 batting average. His RBI total and 41 home runs were the most ever hit by a catcher until Johnny Bench passed those numbers in 1970.

A huge fan favorite at the Dodgers' storied Ebbetts Field, Campanella was the second National League player ever to win three MVP awards (the other was Stan Musial). No other black player won that many MVPs until Barry Bonds did it in 1993.

Roy's career numbers—a .276 batting average with 242 home runs and 856 RBI in 4,205 at-bats in 1,215 games—told only part of the story. He was a magnificent catcher defensively and an astute handler of pitchers. He was also regarded as the heart and soul of the hugely successful Dodgers teams on which he played.

The word was that the stocky five-foot-nine Campy could "hit a pitch a mile," when he got hold of one. That was never truer than in a game in 1950 against the Cincinnati Reds when he hit three balls off Ken Raffensberger over the roof at Crosley Field.

One of his other key assets was his throwing arm, which was often said to be the greatest in baseball history. In his first two seasons, he threw out an amazing 64 percent of the runners who tried to steal a base, at one point going 51 straight games without allowing a stolen base. One season, with his snap throw, he threw out 23 of the 38 runners who tried to steal a base on him. In one game, with the bases loaded and none out, he picked off two base runners.

And he was resilient. He often played despite being injured. Once, he broke a bone in his wrist but continued to play for several weeks before submitting to surgery. During his 10 years in the big leagues, he played in 100 or more games every season, and hit 30 or more home runs in four seasons. Campy was called a "take-charge guy" who ran the game from behind the plate, yet Dodgers vice president Fresco Thompson called him "the most relaxed ballplayer I've ever seen."

Off the field, Campanella was a humorous, gentle, unassuming man, but once he went behind the plate he became a brilliant, extremely tough catcher who defensively was about as good as anybody who ever wore a mask and chest protector. So quick and agile was he that he was sometimes called "The Cat," despite his large size. He possessed a rocketlike throwing arm, could catch pitches that most backstops would have merely waved at, and had a masterful ability to call a game.

"Just seeing him back there [behind the plate] made you a better pitcher," said Dodgers ace hurler Johnny Podres, who won the third and the deciding seventh game with Campanella behind the plate as the Dodgers won the first World Series in team history.

Campanella was part of another remarkable situation in baseball history. Over the five-decade period from 1948 to 1998, three of the Dodgers' primary catchers came from the Philadelphia area. Mike Scioscia of Springfield, later the highly successful manager of the Los Angeles Angels, and Mike Piazza of Phoenixville, a 2016 Hall of Fame inductee, were the others.

In January 1958, the year that the Dodgers moved from Brooklyn to Los Angeles, Campanella's career came to a tragic end. While he was driving home one night, his car skidded off a slippery road, plowed into a pole, and flipped over, leaving Roy pinned behind the steering wheel. The 36-year-old catcher suffered multiple injuries, including fractures in his vertebrae, and was paralyzed from the neck down.

The accident was front-page news throughout the country. One of the best and most revered athletes in the United States had been victimized by a devastating disaster, and there was shock and sadness everywhere. Campanella spent the rest of his life as a quadriplegic, navigating in a wheelchair, although for many years he would go to spring training with the Dodgers at Vero Beach, Florida, and work with the team's young catchers.

On May 7, 1959, the now Los Angeles Dodgers held an exhibition game to benefit Campanella, playing against the New York Yankees at the Los Angeles Coliseum. With the enthusiastic support of Hollywood celebrities, some 93,103 spectators packed the stadium. Before the game, Reese pushed Campy in his wheelchair onto the field, where a parade of speakers preceded Roy's turn at the microphone.

Roy tearfully thanked the fans and his friends and family for their support. And then he turned toward the stands and called out to a very special person in his life. That person's name was Biz Mackey, and he was by then a longtime resident of Los Angeles.

"When I learned where he was living, I wasted no time contacting him and invited him to have dinner with me," Campanella wrote many years later. "I hadn't seen him in 15 years."

One of the "nicest things" that happened to him at the game, Roy added, "was seeing my friend, tutor, and first manager, Biz Mackey." Campanella called on Mackey to stand up and take a bow. "This is the man that gave me all of the techniques in my catching ability, that started me out at a young age," Campy told spectators. As the crowd roared its approval, Mackey was nearly overcome with emotion.

In 1969, Campanella's brilliant career was justly rewarded with his election to the Baseball Hall of Fame. Only Robinson, among black players, preceded him to the Hall. When Roy received the honor, there was no doubt that the name of Biz Mackey was never too far from his thoughts. After all, if hadn't been for Mackey, Campanella, who died in 1993, might never have made it to Cooperstown.

This house, at 1127 East 27th Street, was the Mackeys' home in Los Angeles. (Biz Mackey Foundation.)

◆ ◆ ◆

9

◆ ◆ ◆

A LONG-OVERDUE INDUCTION
INTO THE HALL OF FAME

ven as late as 1947, Mackey was still making an occasional appearance in a game. That year, in his final season as manager of the Newark Eagles, Mackey played in eight games.

His final trip to the plate occurred on August 24 of that season. Sending himself to the plate as a pinch-hitter, Mackey was given an intentional walk. As intended, cheers from the stands showered down on the 50-year-old Negro League icon.

Then at the end of the season, Effa Manley relieved Mackey of his duties as the Eagles manager.

When Mackey's career ended in 1947, he had a cumulative .327 batting average with 1,087 hits, 68 home runs, 702 RBI, and 567 runs in 3,326 at-bats. Overall, Mackey played in 947 league games, making just 146 errors during his career. Between 1933 and 1947, he played in five East-West All-Star games.

He may have been done with Negro League baseball, but Mackey was still not ready to retire from the game. Subsequently,

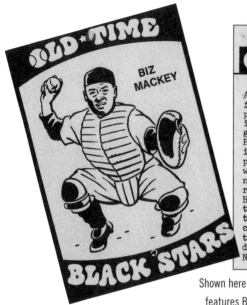

27 **RALEIGH (BIZ) MACKEY** C

A tremendous hitter and a fierce competitor, with a powerful throwing arm, Biz is regarded as perhaps Negro ball's finest catcher. He began with the San Antonio Giants in 1918 and was playing 30 years later. Biz was a switch hitter who did not have running speed but recorded some high averages. He played many years with the Hilldale club. Mackey taught Roy Campanella about catching and as manager of the Newark Eagles aided in developing Larry Doby, Don Newcombe and Monte Irvin.

Shown here is one of the rare baseball cards that features Biz Mackey. (Biz Mackey Foundation.)

he moved to Los Angeles, California, and in 1948 he played with a barnstorming team called the San Francisco Sea Lions.

By that time, Mackey had finally met up with his former lover Lucille. The two had met during Biz's first trip to Japan, had fallen in love, and had corresponded for a while after Mackey returned to the United States. They lost touch when World War II began, but, after the war was over, Lucille, the daughter of an African American father and a Japanese mother, moved from Japan to San Francisco. The two crossed paths and began dating again. Soon they got married and settled into a home in the Los Angeles suburb of Inglewood, California.

Mackey had previously barnstormed in California a number of times earlier in his career. With the team sponsored by Shell Oil Company, he had played a team that included Bob Meusel, Babe Herman, Tony Lazzeri, and Ping Bodie during the winter of

1928. With no Negro League in 1929, he had also played in California against a team that included Jimmie Foxx, Al Simmons, Ed Rommell, and Lefty Grove. Even in his 50s, Biz continued to play with barnstorming teams and in the California Winter League once he moved to the West Coast. Having already played in that league during the winter months of several of his years in the Negro Leagues, he eventually wound up playing in a record 26 seasons in California, where he had the sixth-highest batting average ever, with a .366 mark with 28 home runs and a record 62 doubles.

At about the same time, Mackey took a job as a forklift operator. In his community, he had friends who had also played Negro League baseball. Along the way, other family members, including his brother Ray, had also moved to the Los Angeles area. Biz's older brother Ernest had passed away some years earlier, but Ernest's grandson, Fletcher, an artist, stayed in Houston, where Biz often visited.

In another family matter that wasn't well known, one of Biz's girlfriends had given birth to a baby girl. Later, in 1950, when that baby girl had grown up, she gave birth to a boy, who would turn out to be Biz's only grandchild. His name was Riley Mackey Odoms, and eventually he would grow up to be an outstanding football player. Odoms played first at the University of Houston before spending 12 years (1972–1983) in the National Football League as a tight end with the Denver Broncos, where he was a four-time Pro Bowl selection and a two-time All-Pro player.

Mackey often talked about his love for the West, especially how he was so close to scenic mountains and a beautiful ocean. It was a lifestyle that had been missing through his early years, but now he was reaping the benefits of a whole different and enjoyable existence without the constant pressure of his previous career. But, as John Holway noted, it was tragic that professional baseball could not find a place for him after his playing days, just as it was tragic that it could not find a place for him in its most prominent league. Holway reflected, "His immense gifts as a teacher and coach were squandered by the game that also turned its back on his talents as a player."

Many parties throughout Mackey's life had promoted those gifts in the hopes of getting him a chance to play in the big leagues, especially New York's *Daily Worker*, which waged a relentless campaign for integrating Major League Baseball starting in the mid-1930s. Even as late as 1943, it had called for an MLB tryout for Mackey, Willie Wells, Kenny Washington, and several others. "I'm so sorry that they [MLB] never got the chance to know precisely how good they were," said Monte Irvin.

"I was born too soon," Mackey was quoted as saying in the *Long Beach* (California) *Press-Telegram* in 1949, two years after his last Negro League game. "In our day, we didn't get the chance that Robinson, Doby, Paige, and the others are now getting to show what they can do in the majors. What wouldn't Bullet [Joe Rogan] and I have given to have had a chance."

Tears reportedly dripped down his cheeks as he reiterated, "I was born 30 years too soon." To that, New York Giants manager John McGraw added: "There's a great catcher, as good as any in baseball today. If I could've whitewashed him, I'd have him on my club today."

Mackey died on September 22, 1965, in Los Angeles, less than four months after driving his 1964 Pontiac Bonneville to Houston to visit his grandson. Biz was still working and driving a forklift when he died. He was buried in the city's Evergreen

Cemetery with his entire name, including "Biz," engraved on the tombstone. Preceded by Lucille's death, Mackey's passing at the age of 68 ended what had been a fulfilling life, highlighted by his glittering career in baseball. A story in the *Los Angeles Sentinel* said that black baseball's "dean of catchers had died."

The crowning achievement of Mackey's career came 41 years after he had passed away. In 2006, Mackey was inducted into the Baseball Hall of Fame at Cooperstown. It was a fitting climax to a career that had begun in the cotton fields of Texas nearly a century earlier.

While Jackie Robinson had been inducted into the Hall of Fame in 1962 and Roy Campanella had earned a spot in the baseball shrine in 1969, there was a growing clamor to induct players who had performed only in the Negro Leagues as well. Although few in baseball agreed with that idea, many feeling that the Hall should be just for Major Leaguers, one who was in favor of admitting Negro League players was the great Boston Red Sox slugger Ted Williams.

When he was inducted into the Hall of Fame in 1966, Williams surprised his audience by making an unforgettable stand during his acceptance speech, urging the Hall to induct former Negro League greats. No one had ever made this argument in such a public statement at such a prestigious baseball event.

"Inside this building are plaques dedicated to baseball men of all generations, and I'm privileged to join them," Williams said. "Baseball gives every American boy a chance to excel. Not just to be as good as someone else, but to be better than someone else. This is the nature of man and the nature of the game. And I've been a very lucky guy to have worn a baseball uniform, and I hope that some day the names of Satchel Paige and Josh

After speaking at Biz's induction into the Hall of Fame, Ray Mackey III (second from right) accepts his great-uncle's Hall of Fame plaque. Joining him (from left) are Hall of Fame officers Dale Petrosky and Jane Forbes Clark and baseball commissioner Bud Selig. (Biz Mackey Foundation.)

Gibson in some way can be added as a symbol of the great Negro players who are not here, only because they were not given a chance."

Williams's stunning statement made an immediate impression. "His speech had an impact," Monte Irvin was quoted as saying in the book *Ted Williams: A Tribute*. "He did change some minds. The writers picked up on it, and some of the powers-that-be at the Hall of Fame had to kind of perk up and take notice."

One writer who did was *Washington Post* sports editor and columnist Shirley Povich. "The fact is that Ted Williams launched the whole movement for the inclusion of Negro League players into the Hall of Fame at Cooperstown," he wrote.

The movement gained momentum, and ultimately, the Baseball Writers' Association of America, which was responsible for annually electing new members to the Hall, was strongly in favor of the suggestion. "Until now, there has been one failing and the baseball writers intend that this be rectified," said BBWAA president Dick Young, a columnist for the *New York Post*, at the Hall's 1969 induction ceremony.

"Nobody questions the credentials of these great baseball players on my right," he added. "They all belong. But we do ask the question[s] 'Why should Waite Hoyt and Stanley Coveleski be in the Hall of Fame and not Satchel Paige? Why should Roy Campanella be in the Hall of Fame, and not Josh Gibson?' There are other men, great ballplayers, who certainly have a place in this shrine."

Another person strongly in favor of that view was baseball commissioner Bowie Kuhn. In 1970, Kuhn held a meeting in his New York office to discuss the idea. Those who attended included National League president Ford Frick, Hall of Fame president Paul Kerr, baseball writers Young and Jack Lang, and members of Kuhn's staff, including Monte Irvin.

Years later, Kuhn described the meeting in his book *Hardball: The Education of a Baseball Commissioner.* "The meeting was heated and unpleasant," Kuhn wrote. "Frick and Kerr took the negative position. Young was passionate and unrelenting in his support of admitting black players."

As a result of the forceful disagreements, Kuhn said that he would "slip around their flank and look for an opening." In 1971, he formed a committee of "Negro League experts" who would identify the best Negro League players and recommend that they get elected to the Hall of Fame.

Even that plan met with strong opposition. "A predictable furor ensued," Kuhn wrote. "Cries of 'Jim Crow' were heard. They said we were again treating players separately, putting them through a back door in Cooperstown. Jackie Robinson, the NAACP, and all sorts of activist groups spoke out in protest."

Although he was personally attacked, Kuhn refused to give in. Accordingly, he appointed a 10-member committee to pursue his plan. The committee consisted of ex-players including Campanella, Judy Johnson, and Irvin; African American writers Sam Lacy and Wendell Smith; and prominent sports and Negro League executives such as Eddie Gottlieb and Alex Pompez.

The committee was allowed to select only one player per year, and it didn't take long to make its first choice. In the summer of 1971, Satchel Paige was inducted into the Hall of Fame.

That year, Williams once again made his case for Negro League players while accepting a brotherhood award at Howard University.

"As I look back on my career, I am thankful that I was given the chance to play baseball," Williams said. "It's about the only thing I could do, and I've thought of this many times: what would have happened to me if I hadn't had a chance to play baseball? A chill goes up my back when I think I might have been denied this if I had been black."

As it turned out, by 1977, Buck Leonard, Josh Gibson, Irvin, Cool Papa Bell, Johnson, Oscar Charleston, Martin Dihigo, and John Henry (Pop) Lloyd had also been inducted into the Hall of Fame. In the ensuing years, more players were chosen for the honor. By 2001, the number had reached 18.

Then, in 2006, the Hall of Fame held one of the most noteworthy inductions in its long history. The event was the culmi-

nation of a long procedure that had begun in 2001, when Major
League Baseball had provided a grant of $250,000 to research
eligible Negro League players.

Led by Negro League historians Larry Lester, Dick Clark,
and Dr. Lawrence Hogan, a diverse group of more than 50
authors, historians, and researchers conducted an unmatched
study of Negro League players and their statistics, drawing on
some 3,000 day-to-day records culled from 128 newspapers,
box scores, and many other historical references dating back to
the early 1920s. The result was an 800-page report that com-
prised what was called "the most comprehensive compilation
of statistics on the Negro League that had ever been accumulated."

A committee of 12 Negro League historians was then appointed to produce a list of candidates for the Hall. Some 94
names made the list. Then a five-man screening committee that
included Lester, Clark, Hogan, Adrian Burgos, and Jim Over-
myer narrowed the list to 39. Ultimately, a voting committee,
chaired by former baseball commissioner Fay Vincent and including Hall of Fame executives and Negro League historians,
chose 17 players and executives for election into the Hall.

"Our committee was, of course, mindful of the historic significance of our assignment," Vincent later wrote. "I am proud of
the process we followed, and of the extraordinary devotion to the
task the members exhibited."

"We were aware the election would cause debate," Vincent
continued, "and some have been loudly critical of aspects of our
decisions. But I believe such disagreements demonstrate that as
baseball fans, we care for our beloved game, and we desire it to
be perfect in all respects."

One of those elected was Biz Mackey. The players inducted, each of whom had to get 75 percent of the votes from the
12-member committee, also included Negro League stars Ray
Brown, Willard Brown, Andy Cooper, Mule Suttles, Cristobal
Torriente, and Jud Wilson, plus pre–Negro League players Louis
Santop, Frank Grant, Pete Hill, Jose Mendez, and Ben Taylor as
well as executives Effa Manley, Alex Pompez, Cum Posey, Sol
White, and J. L. Wilkinson. Manley was the first woman elected
to the Hall of Fame.

"I applaud the National Baseball Hall of Fame for conduct-
ing this special study," said then commissioner Allan (Bud) Selig.
"Major League Baseball is proud to have played a part in a process that has corrected some of those omissions."

The inductions took place on July 30, 2006. Since all 17 en-
trants had passed away, the speakers for the group were former
Negro Leaguer Buck O'Neil and Robinson's daughter, Sharon.
Family members accepted the awards for the inductees, which
that day also included former big-league pitcher Bruce Sutter.

Biz's great-nephew Ray Mackey III was invited to the ceremony to accept the award. Other members of the Mackey family were also present, including Biz's grandson, former National
Football League star Riley Mackey Odoms.

"It's been a long time coming, and your great uncle is very
deserving of his honor," Jeff Idelson, then the Hall of Fame vice
president of communications and education, wrote to Ray. "I'm
so happy for you and your family."

"I just wish he could be here to see this," said Mackey while
accepting his forebearer's honor. "He overcame oppression, the
great depressions, and racism, and now, years after his death, his
greatness is finally coming to fruition."

For Biz Mackey, who had broken in as Santop's backup and had gone on to a brilliant career, the induction was long overdue. The man who many called one of baseball's greatest catchers, and who Ty Cobb once said was "one of the most intense competitors the national pastime has ever known," had finally been awarded a well-deserved place in the hallowed shrine of baseball.

In 2011, Mackey was honored again when he became only the second Negro League player (Judy Johnson was the first) inducted into the Philadelphia Sports Hall of Fame. Once more, Biz Mackey was honored for being one of baseball's greatest players.

APPENDIX

◆ ◆ ◆

Biz Mackey's Year-by-Year
Negro League Statistics

Year	Team	G	AB	R	H	HR	RBI	BA
1920	Indianapolis ABCs	35	128	15	37	1	20	.289
1921	Indianapolis ABCs	54	171	30	62	7	50	.310
1922	Indianapolis ABCs	75	269	48	102	8	85	.382
1923	Hilldale Daisies	45	171	28	71	4	48	.415
1924	Hilldale Daisies	80	321	57	104	4	46	.324
1925	Hilldale Daisies	68	235	53	82	7	57	.349
1926	Hilldale Daisies	86	310	60	104	10	83	.335
1927	Hilldale Daisies, Homestead Grays	31	107	28	34	3	24	.318
1928	Hilldale Daisies, Baltimore Black Sox	57	218	45	76	4	42	.349
1929	Hilldale Daisies	32	118	20	39	2	19	.331
1930	Hilldale Daisies, Baltimore Black Sox	37	130	28	53	5	38	.408
1931	Hilldale Daisies	51	186	37	64	5	41	.344
1932	Did Not Play							
1933	Philadelphia Stars	22	76	7	22	0	13	.289
1934	Philadelphia Stars	2	73	7	23	2	15	.315
1935	Philadelphia Stars	44	155	18	39	2	23	.252
1936	Baltimore Elite Giants	31	117	16	34	1	22	.291
1937	Baltimore Elite Giants	27	83	8	20	0	6	.241
1938	Baltimore Elite Giants	29	106	16	30	0	19	.283
1939	Baltimore Elite Giants, Newark Eagles	27	80	9	27	1	12	.338
1940	Newark Eagles	37	123	17	38	1	25	.309
1941	Newark Eagles	25	65	7	16	0	8	.246
1942– 1944								
1945	Newark Eagles	11	35	3	6	1	4	.171
1946	Newark Eagles	8	7	0	1	0	0	.143
1947	Newark Eagles	9	18	0	3	0	3	.167
Career		947	3326	567	1087	68	702	.327

Source: Statistics compiled by Negro League Researchers and Authors Group, Larry Lester and Dick Clark.

SOURCES

◆ ◆ ◆

BOOKS

Biddle, Daniel, and Murray Dubin. *Tasting Freedom: Octavius Catto and the Battle for Equality in Civil War America*. Philadelphia: Temple University Press, 2010.

Brashler, Williams. *Josh Gibson: A Life in the Negro Leagues*. New York: Harper and Row, 1978.

Campanella, Roy, *It's Good to Be Alive*. Boston: Little Brown, 1959.

Cieradkowski, Gary Joseph. *The League of Outsider Baseball*. New York: Touchstone, 2015.

Clark, Dick, and Larry Lester, eds. *The Negro Leagues Book*. Phoenix, AZ: Society of American Baseball Research, 1994.

Fitts, Robert K. *Banzai Babe Ruth: Baseball, Espionage, and Assassination during the 1934 Tour of Japan*. Lincoln: University of Nebraska Press, 2012.

Gay, Timothy M. *Satch, Dizzy and Rapid Robert: The Wild Saga of Interracial Baseball before Jackie Robinson*. New York: Simon and Schuster, 2010.

Glenn, Stanley. *Don't Let Anyone Take Your Joy Away: An Inside Look at Negro League Baseball and Its Legacy*. Bloomington, IN: iUniverse, Inc., 2006.

Golenbock, Peter. *Bums: An Oral History of the Brooklyn Dodgers*. New York: G. P. Putnam's Sons, 1984.

Guthrie-Shimizu, Sayuri. *Transpacific Field of Dreams*. Chapel Hill: University of North Carolina Press, 2012.

Heaphy, Leslie A. *The Negro Leagues, 1869–1960*. Jefferson, NC: McFarland, 2003.

Hogan, Lawrence. *Shades of Glory: The Negro Leagues and the Story of African American Baseball.* Washington, DC: National Geographic, 2006.

Holway, John. *Blackball Stars: Negro League Pioneers.* New York: Carrol and Graf Publishers, 1988.

———. *Voices from the Great Black Baseball Leagues.* New York: Dodd, Mead, 1975.

Kuhn, Bowie. *Hardball: The Education of a Baseball Commissioner.* Lincoln, NE: Bison Books, 1997.

Lanctot, Neil. *Campy: The Two Lives of Roy Campanella.* New York: Simon and Schuster, 2011.

———. *Fair Dealing and Clean Playing: The Hilldale Club and the Development of Black Professional Baseball, 1910–1932.* Jefferson, NC: McFarland, 1994.

———. *Negro League Baseball: The Rise and Ruin of a Black Institution.* Philadelphia: University of Pennsylvania Press, 2004.

Lester, Larry. *Baseball's First Colored World Series.* Jefferson, NC: McFarland, 2006.

Luke, Bob. *The Most Famous Woman in Black Baseball.* Washington, DC: Potomac Books, 2011.

Montville, Leigh. *Ted Williams: The Biography of an American Hero.* New York: Doubleday, 2004.

Peterson, Robert. *Only the Ball Was White: A History of Legendary Black Players and All-Black Professional Teams.* Oxford: Oxford University Press, 1970.

Prime, Jim, and Bill Nowlin, eds. *Ted Williams: A Tribute.* Indianapolis: Masters Press, 1997.

Ribowsky, Mark. *A Complete History of the Negro Leagues, 1884 to 1955.* Secaucus, NJ: Carol Publishing Group, 1995.

Riley, James A. *The Biographical Encyclopedia of the Negro Baseball Leagues.* New York: Carroll and Graf Publishers, 1994.

Rogosin, Donn. *Invisible Men: Life in Baseball's Negro Leagues.* New York: Atheneum, 1983.

Threston, Christopher. *The Integration of Baseball in Philadelphia.* Jefferson, NC: McFarland, 2003.

Veeck, Bill. *Veeck as in Wreck.* Chicago: University of Chicago Press, 1962.

Vincent, Faye. *The Last Commissioner: A Baseball Valentine.* New York: Simon and Schuster, 2002.

Westcott, Rich. *Diamond Greats: Profiles and Interviews with 65 of Baseball's History Makers.* Westport, CT: Meckler Books, 1988.

———. *The Mogul: Eddie Gottlieb, Philadelphia Sports Legend and Pro Basketball Pioneer.* Philadelphia: Temple University Press, 2008.

White, Sol. *History of Colored Base Ball.* Lincoln: University of Nebraska Press, 1995.

ARTICLES

Gates, Jim. "Biz and Hank's Wonderful Adventure, Memories and Dreams."
National Baseball Hall of Fame, 2006.
King, David. "Baseball: Late Negro Leaguer Mackey Joins Hall of Fame." *San
Antonio Express-News*, July 30, 2006.
Sayama, Kazuo. "Black Gentle Giants." *Tokyo Baseball Magazine*, 1986.
———. "Their Throws Were like Arrows—How a Black Team Spurred Pro
Ball in Japan." *Baseball Research Journal* (Society for American Base-
ball Research) 16 (1987): 85–88.
Thomas, Dexter. "The Secret History of Black Baseball Players in Japan."
NPR, July 14, 2015. Available at http://www.npr.org/sections/codeswitch
/2015/07/14/412880758/the-secret-history-of-black-baseball-players-in-
japan.

MASTER'S THESIS

Smith, Courtney. "A Faded Memory." Master's thesis, Lehigh University,
2002.

VIDEO

Ferrett, Andrew. *19th Century Baseball*. 2009.
Stephenson, Dan. *They Said We Couldn't Play: An Oral History of the Philadelphia Stars*. Philadelphia: Philadelphia Phillies, 2012.

NEWSPAPERS AND OTHER SOURCES

Afro-American
Amsterdam News
Baseball World
Daily Worker (New York)
Delaware County Daily Times
Free Library of Philadelphia
Japan Times
Kansas City Royals Scouting Report
Long Beach (California) *Press-Telegram*
Los Angeles Sentinel
MajorLeagueBaseball.com
National Baseball Hall of Fame
NegroLeagueBaseball.com
Negro League Baseball Museum
Newark Herald

New York Post
Philadelphia Daily News
Philadelphia Evening Bulletin
Philadelphia Inquirer
Philadelphia Tribune
Pittsburgh Courier
San Antonio Express-News
Seamheads.com (Negro League database)
The Sporting News
Springfield (Delaware County) Library
St. Louis Post-Dispatch
Temple University, Charles Blockson Afro-American Collection
Temple University, Urban Archives
Washington Post
Washington Tribune
Wikipedia

INDEX

◆ ◆ ◆

Veeck, Bill, 51, 52
Venezuela, 146
Vernon, Mickey, 129, 130
Vero Beach, FL, 150
Vincent, Fay, 163

Waco, TX, 32
Waddell, Rube, 46, 47
Wagner, Honus, 63
Walberg, Rube, 71
Wakahara, Shozo, 105
Walcott, Joe, 50
Walker, Moses (Fleetwood), 45
Walker, Jim, 61
Warfield, Frank, 64, 67–69
Warminster, PA, 92
Washington, Kenny, 158
Washington, Namon, 69
Washington, Ted, 53
Washington Elite Giants, 90, 118
Washington Senators, 129
Wells, Willie, 84, 86, 103, 125, 128, 130, 158
West Philadelphia, 51, 121
West Philadelphia Giants, 50
White, Sol, 40, 45, 47, 164
Wilkinson, J. L., 164
Williams, Marvin, 94

Williams, Nish, 141
Williams, Ted, 159, 160, 162
Williamsport, PA, 45
Wilmington, DE, 13, 46, 48–50, 61, 132
Wilson, Horace, 100
Wilson, Ernest (Jud), 40, 81, 164
Wilson, Rollo, 64, 85, 87
Wilson, Tom, 118, 120, 145
Winters, Jesse (Nip), 49, 65, 66, 74, 89
Woodside Hotel, 140
World Colored Championship, 44, 46
World Series, 11, 41, 49, 74, 80, 89, 147, 150
World War II, 94, 108, 111–113, 127, 156
Wright, Bill, 119
Wyncote, PA, 41

Yale University, 101
Yancey, Bill, 76
Yankee Stadium, 80, 86, 121
Yeadon, PA, 48, 49, 59, 62, 69
York, PA, 45, 82
Young, Dick, 161

Zenimura, Kenso, 103, 112

A leading authority on Philadelphia baseball, **Rich Westcott** is the author of 25 previous books. A newspaper and magazine writer, an editor for more than 40 years, and a former president of the Philadelphia Sports Writers Association, he has written for numerous national publications. He was the founding publisher of the newspaper *Phillies Report*, which covered the team for 14 years, and has appeared in 10 documentaries about baseball history. He is an inductee into four halls of fame.